Hepting

A Family History

1750 - 2020

Author
Sandra M Read

First published in Great Britain in 2021

ISBN: 9798512520024

This book is based on facts obtained through extensive research and family memories.

Acknowledgements and Dedications

My special thanks go to my late mother and father, Barbara and Bill Hepting for preserving the family photographs and information used in this book.

A sincere thank you to the late Jim Hepting for all his early research, documents, family memories and photographs that he shared with me and for starting the family search that has culminated in this book.

Thanks also to the late Sidney Robert Hepting for his part in the early research. Many thanks also to all those named who freely shared photographs, information and family memories for inclusion into this book: the late Ann Barbara (Hepting) Saville, Sylvia (Hepting) (Pickley) Kelly, the daughters of Janet (Hepting) Sewell, Joan and Jane. Also to all my cousins who shared their information and photographs: to Carol and Pearl who provided information and photographs of the Bedford family and to Gunter Hepting and his parents, our distant relatives who live in Germany today, for their information and photographs.

Last but not least my greatest thanks to my husband for reading and editing each draft of this book.

This book is dedicated to the wider Hepting family. I hope that you will enjoy reading about the lives of our ancestors and relatives covering the last two hundred and fifty years. For future generations the book will provide starting points for those who would like to continue the family research into the many connected families through the ages.

CONTENTS

Introduction

The origin of our history

This book tells the history of one branch of the Hepting family. The journey begins with Gertrud Kirner and her illegitimate son who was born in Eisenbach, a village in the Black Forest of Germany and concludes with the large family that we are today in the UK.

According to a German genealogist, who Jim Hepting employed, the surname of Hepting is said to have originated in the small village of Ewattingen in Southern Germany. It was the name given to people who left the small village and settled elsewhere. There doesn't appear to be any documentary evidence to support this or of when this first occurred. The surname of Hepting is found in Urach, Baden, South West Germany as far back as 1559 but the true origins of the name have not been verified to date.

Our branch of the Hepting family traces back, through the male line, to Anton Kirner born in 1819. It's a long and interesting history covering over two hundred years. The birth of one has produced many, many families in the UK and around the world who can trace their heritage directly back to the Hepting/Kirner families of the Black Forest in Germany. This book concentrates on the eight generations of the branch of the Hepting family originating from Anton (Kirner) Hepting. This account has been compiled from information and documents collected over the last thirty-five years.

The research was carried out by Jim Hepting, Bill Hepting, their brother Sidney Hepting and myself.

Jim, Bill and Sidney made frequent trips to London to research and obtain documents before the information was available on the internet. Before Jim Hepting passed away I said that I would put the information collected by us all into a family history book. This would ensure that all the years of research, carried out by us all, would not be wasted and would be available to those who want to learn about their ancestral family and their background.

I hope that this book will show something of our ancestors lives, so that we can understand them and to know where and how they lived with wars, prejudice, hunger, poverty, hardship and loss in their lives. Despite all the hardships the family survived, grew and flourished.

The Black Forest

Our history begins deep in the Black Forest of southern Germany, in the village of Eisenbach.

It is a picturesque region with the River Rhine enclosing this corner of the Black Forest (Schwarzwald). Donaueschingen, a village nine miles (15km) to the east of Eisenbach, is the start of the Danube river. Six and a half miles (10km) to the south west is Lake Titisee and approximately thirty-seven miles (60km) south is the Swiss border. The landscape has beautiful, rolling green hills, valleys and meadows with wooded hillsides and small hamlets and villages peppered among them. The terrain is steep in this area and on the northern borders there are high mountains and waterfalls.

The town of Titisee-Neustadt is just north east of Lake Titisee where today there is a spa hotel, a golf course and grab ski lifts nearby. There is a train service from Freiburg to Titisee-Neustadt and beyond which also stops at Lake Titisee. There are many spas, lidos and outdoor leisure facilities in this region and the area is said to have an almost Mediterranean climate.

Freiberg is the nearest major town and the administrative capital of the Black Forest. Reputed to be the sunniest place in Germany, it's definitely a solar city and has been described as the home of solar panels. Ninety-five per cent of the city's energy is from renewable sources. Freiberg lies twenty-seven miles (43km) to the west of Eisenbach.

The area is scenically stunning and so it's hardly

surprising that the area is a popular holiday spot year-round, with walkers, hikers and skiers.

Freiberg is a picturesque, vibrant and colourful university city, with an old centre of cobbled streets. The minster as well as the grand town hall buildings can be found in the market place where a market is still held every day. Alongside many of the city's streets there are water run-off channels from the River Dreisam, these channels are known as Bächle. Legend has it that if you accidentally slip into these ankle deep channels you will marry a Freiberger. Back in the middle ages livestock would drink from the channels and they were also used to put out fires in the wooden buildings of the time.

On the cobbles, outside shops, you can see symbols in mosaic tiling which indicate what each shop sells. Many bars, cafes and restaurants with outside tables line these streets and in the summer months it's hard to find a seat! The city and the surrounding areas are very easy to get around too with good transport links.

The Black Forest - centre of cuckoo clockmaking

The oldest clock making factory in the world is located in Schonwald, a small village not far from Eisenbach. It was here that it was initially believed that the first cuckoo clock was made in the Black Forest in 1733 by Franz Ketterer. This is debatable as the Swiss claim that they made the first cuckoo clock. It is thought that Franz Ketterer was the first to put the 'cuckoo' sound into the cuckoo clock by using bellows. Two of the world's largest cuckoo clocks are located in Schonach, a few kilometres (miles) north of Schonwald. In Furtwangen, a short distance north of Eisenbach, the old clock making school is now the German Clock Museum and has the world's largest collection of historical clocks with over 4,000 now housed there. The Hotel-Bad in Eisenbach is run by Hubert Worsthorn and hosts an annual fayre for clock enthusiasts.

In the mid 1800's, the Grand Duchy of Baden donated some land and a building for a school of clockmaking to be established. The school taught mathematics and drawing and painting for clock design and clock making. Early cuckoo clocks had wooden painted faces rather than the carved faces we see today. At the opening of the school a competition was launched to design a clock and the winning design was that of the cuckoo clock we see today.

The Grand Duke paid for and supported the school in order to raise the standard of the clocks being made in the area. He wanted to enhance the reputation of the local clockmakers and encourage trade for the local businesses. The clocks made at Furtwangen, and in the villages and towns locally, were distributed across the world, including America, Russia, England, Scotland and India.

Originally the clocks would have been made with wooden movements but were later made with brass and metal works which made them more accurate and durable.

A brief history of the region

Before the unification of the German states on 18th January 1871, Germany was a collection of sovereign and Holy Roman Emperor states under different rulers.

Costs and taxes were high for transporting goods between states and charges were levied at each border through which food and goods crossed. This increased the cost of goods and food at their destination by so much that they were beyond the reach of most people.

The economy and the people suffered in the 1700's and early 1800's and left people across most of Europe starving and desolate. Many thousands died and families were left struggling to survive. Babies were christened within twenty four hours of their birth because so many died within days or at a very young age. Nutrition was very poor due to the lack of food. The fact that death was common in the young would not have diminished the pain felt by the parents or the families.

There were grave food shortages right across Europe during the war years of the 1700's and up to the middle to late 1800's. The lack of food was so serious that the heads of Europe at that time formed a coalition to try to feed those that were starving and dying through lack of food.

Disease was rife and in some cities cholera was also thriving. Most of the farmers from the small villages would have grown the bulk of their food in summer and no doubt kept chickens for food and eggs in addition. In the winter months when they were unable to grow crops they would turn to their winter trades such as clockmaking, woodworking, furniture making, carving and others to earn some money to live through the winter months which could be harsh.

Due to the economy and instability of the region and the restrictive legislation governing marriage and having children, countless people left their homelands from across the German states. They hoped to find better lives and to further their opportunities for trade. Many took up apprenticeships outside the region emigrating to Hungary, the UK and the USA whilst others went further afield to Australia and New Zealand.

Parents would save what money they could to send the eldest son to an apprenticeship abroad. There was only room for so many clockmakers in the region and due to the hardships it was felt their eldest son would benefit from going abroad where there were more opportunities for their business.

Emigrating was not seen as an easy option. The cost of travel and the apprenticeship had to be paid for by the apprentice. No salary or expenses were given in return for any work they did in respect of their apprenticeship. Paying for the documents required to travel and the high risks involved in travelling in those times, both on land and on sea, would have deterred most people. Witnessed and signed documents had to be provided in support of an application to obtain a passport to go abroad. The applicant had to be sponsored and the documents signed by several local people, preferably a dignitary or two, stating that the person had sufficient funds to go and stay for the duration of the apprenticeship.

There was no universal passport that allowed travel either from the German states or, as a citizen of the

Ducal state, between other countries. Each time a citizen of their home state wanted to travel, whether it be out of their state or between other countries e.g. UK to the USA, the citizen would have had to re-apply for more papers and there would be further costs. Everything also had to be done in person by appointment or by letter.

The conditions on the ships on which they sailed were not of today's standards. There were frequent deaths aboard the ships from disease, hunger and squalid conditions, particularly for those paying the bare minimum for their passage.

Ships docked at various ports around the UK, usually at Dover from Hamburg and at Ellis Island in New York for the United States. Despite the difficulties, the journey was considered worth the risks as the opportunities for trading in the bigger cities outside of the German states were greater. Few returned to the Black Forest but most settled in their adopted land. Some also went on to Scotland where the scenery would have been similar to their homeland.

A major city like London in the 1800's would have been quite a shock for someone arriving from the Black Forest.

In some families, brothers, uncles and cousins, had already made the journey to London and would have been able to convey the opportunities for trade, perhaps even offering apprenticeships in their established businesses. The new and plentiful trade in a large city no doubt fuelled the enthusiasm for emigration, despite the unpleasant conditions in London at the time. Life in America and England after 1865, politically and economically, was more stable than in the German states and this would also have been a factor.

In this region of the German states the youngest

son inherited from the parents, not the eldest, as in England. This was to ensure that the property and assets stayed in the family for as long as possible.

The wars between the nations and states had made life hard not least because of the changing politics, loyalties and borders but also because men were drafted to fight, leaving families without the help of their sons to work the land.

The city of Freiberg was documented in the 12th century although the settlement existed before this time and has gone through many changes of rulership in its history. Because of its location it had been invaded, conquered and ruled by the Swedes, Spanish, French, Prussians and Austrians before being given up to the Grand Dukes of Baden in the 1800's. All changed again after unification of the German states in 1871.

During the second world war Freiberg was heavily bombed and as late as November 1944 the old city centre was flattened with only buildings left standing on the outskirts and the minster surviving in the inner city.

Fortunately, unlike other cities across Europe, after the second world war Freiberg was rebuilt in the same style and street plans that existed before the war damage and it therefore retains its original charm and sense of history today. It's not at all evident that the city had been devastated and is now, in part at least, as it would have looked some two hundred years ago. There are of course many new buildings outside of the old centre.

The recording of names in the records

Confusingly, names were shown with various spellings at different times in the Black Forest region. In earlier years you may see the name Anton spelled as Antonius and Antonii, Lorenz as Laurentius and Lorentii,

Gertrud as Gertrudis and Gertrudii. The spellings depended on the laws and ruler of the region at the time. Later documents show the more modern spelling as Anton, Lorenz and Gertrud, more akin to the Swiss or French language. Eisenbach is very close to both the Swiss and French borders.

Surnames can also be difficult to research as misspellings or mis-interpretations occurred then as now. Heitzman may be shown as Haitzman, Hiezmann and other variations! The surname of Hepting in the records is also shown as Hebding, Hepding and Hebting among others. So when researching it's always worth trying different spellings.

The first Christian name of many Catholic children at that time was usually that of a saint and the middle name was the 'called' name. Maria Agatha would be known as Agatha. Both names only being used for official purposes. This also has to be remembered when researching names.

For the purposes of this book I will use the modern spellings, Anton, Lorenz and Gertrud. When looking at documents in any research you may do, you may encounter the variations as mentioned.

Marriages and Family connections

It was common practice for families to marry with the families of neighbouring villages and often the same surnames would recur in successive generations. There may be a Ganter marrying a Hepting in one generation and then a Hepting marrying a Ganter from another branch of the family in another village in either the same generation or the next. By the laws at the time there had to be a fourth degree of blood separation between the couple to be married which meant that first cousins could marry and this was quite common at the time. The local villages of this region, among others, Schonach, Friedenweiler, Furtwangen, Lloffingen, Neustadt, Urach and St. Peter would have many that were inter-related by at least the fourth degree. Marriages would also take place from villages further afield but usually within the local area as distances and the terrain were difficult to cross, particularly in winter. There are still many Hepting, Ganter and Kirner families living in the Black Forest region today.

The religion of the area was Catholic as was the case for the Hepting, Ganter and Kirner families from whom we originate. Most marriages, christenings and burials took place and were registered in the village of Friedenweiler, near the town of Titisee-Neustadt. Marriages, christenings and burials could also take place in the principal city of the region, Freiberg. Family surnames common to this region, among others, are Ketterer, Kirner, Ganter, Beha, Hepting, Heitzman, Duffner and Willman. While researching the family history it was found that many of the families were respected clockmakers, clock carvers and clock case painters and had family connections to one another through the generations.

In Freiberg in 1865, the Ganter Brewery was founded by Louis Ganter and you can see the Ganter beer sign in most bars, restaurants and hotels today in the locale. As of 2016 the brewery is run by Katharina Ganter-Fraschetti and Detlef Frankenberger.

As can be seen from the family trees the surname of Ganter does appear in our early family history. I have not researched a link to the brewery family but I'm sure there must be one, given the liking of a pint or two by most of the family members.

Part One

Hepting

A Family History

Germany

1750 - 1892

The Hepting Family Tree – Germany

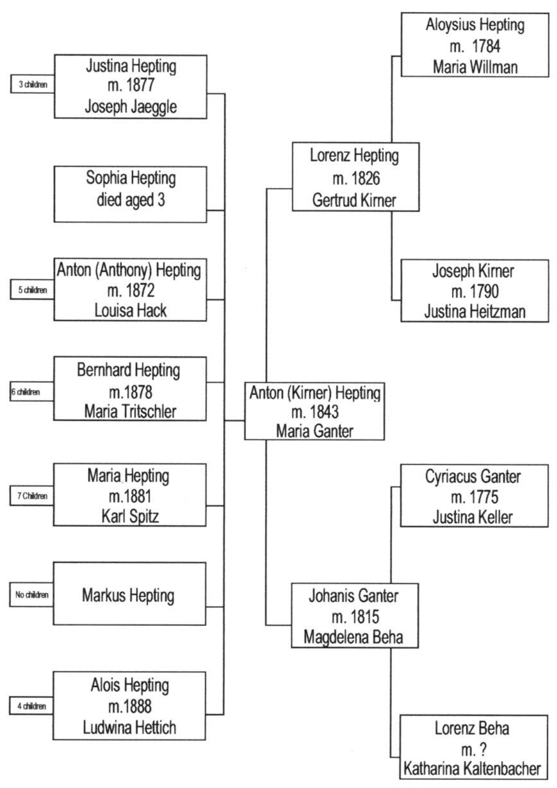

3 children
Justina Hepting
m. 1877
Joseph Jaeggle
Sophia Hepting
died aged 3
5 children
Anton (Anthony) Hepting
m. 1872
Louisa Hack
6 children
Bernhard Hepting
m.1878
Maria Tritschler
7 Children
Maria Hepting
m.1881
Karl Spitz
No children
Markus Hepting
4 children
Alois Hepting
m.1888
Ludwina Hettich
Anton (Kirner) Hepting
m. 1843
Maria Ganter
Lorenz Hepting
m. 1826
Gertrud Kirner
Johanis Ganter
m. 1815
Magdelena Beha
Aloysius Hepting
m. 1784
Maria Willman
Joseph Kirner
m. 1790
Justina Heitzman
Cyriacus Ganter
m. 1775
Justina Keller
Lorenz Beha
m. ?
Katharina Kaltenbacher

Gertrud KIRNER

Although in this book we are looking at the male line of our family, the Hepting line, we must start with Gertrud Kirner, who was christened in Friedenweiler, a village in the Black Forest of southern Germany on 6th March 1797. Gertrud was born to parents Justina Heitzman, born in 1760 and Joseph Kirner, born in 1759. They were married on 9th February 1790.

Gertrud had two older sisters:

Agatha Kirner was born and christened on 27th November 1790. Agatha married Johannes Baptista Haas on 12th January 1824. Johannes was born in 1801 to parents Andreas Haas and Justinae Merk.

I have not found any children of the marriage but it may be that not all the records are available on the internet as yet.

Agatha was buried on 8th October 1858, aged sixty-seven, in Eisenbach.

Johannes Baptista Haas was buried in 1859, aged fifty-eight.

Helena Kirner was born on 8th August 1792 and married Michael Brugger on 21st October 1822. Michael Brugger was born in September 1800 to parents Martin and Gertrud (Tesseig) Brugger. Helena and Michael had a daughter in 1824, naming her Monika.

Monika married Joseph Winterhalder in 1845. Joseph was born in 1815 to parents Andreas Winterhalder and Hellene (Kleiser). After their marriage they lived in Urach, a small hamlet midway between Eisenbach and Furtwangen and in 1849 they had a daughter named

Sophia. Sophia may have been named after Maria and Anton's Hepting's daughter Sophia who died in 1849.

Monika died in February 1851 aged just twenty-six and only six years after her marriage to Joseph. Sadly her two year old daughter Sophia also died that same year in December 1851.

Monika's mother Helena (Kirner) Brugger died in March 1857 aged sixty-four.

Monika's father Michael Brugger remarried the following year to Isabelle Strub in October 1858.

Gertrud and her sisters were born during the last years of the reign of the Holy Roman Empire of the German Nation and a few years before the dissolution in 1806. Gertrud would have had a difficult start in life due to the instability of the area at the time. Many of the sons of farmers would have been called to fight, leaving the family farms or businesses without help to maintain them.

Some German states were concerned about the rising population of the poor classes and so legislation was passed restricting marriage only to those that community authorities considered morally and financially capable of raising a family. Evidence had to be produced that the man had been discharged from military service, that he had an income and property to provide for the family and could also make provision for any children should the parents die before the children were grown. There was also a charge made for the documents and assessment by the authorities. This meant that most people would not have been able to marry as they would not have been able to meet these requirements. Instead of bringing down the number of births though, couples just went ahead and had the children without marrying so the plan of the authorities didn't have the desired effect.

I believe that it was due to this legislation that Gertrud gave birth to her children illegitimately. Gertrud's first child was a daughter, born at home in Eisenbach on 27th February 1817 and christened Gertrudis. The christening and registration took place at Friedenweiler on 28th February 1817. The original birth record shows this as an illegitimate birth to single mother Gertrud Kirner, no father was noted. However on the 4th March 1817, just four days after her christening, Gertrudis Kirner died. This was sadly common at the time, due to lack of nutrition, poor hygiene and disease.

The following year, late in 1818, Gertrud was expecting her second child. Gertrud, now aged twenty-two, gave birth to a boy on 3rd June 1819. Gertrud named her son Anton. Anton is the first male ancestor that we can be sure we are descended from. Anton was baptised and the birth registered on 4th June 1819 at Friedenweiler. Again, no father was recorded on the birth register and a copy of the original record shows that Anton was born illegitimately to single mother Gertrud.

This book of our ancestry will follow Anton and his descendants.

Life was difficult and it was not an easy time to bring up children. However, as Gertrud's father Joseph was a master clockmaker he may have been in a better position than most to provide for his family, although another mouth to feed would not have been easy.

Anton's father may have been present and living with and supporting him but this is unknown. In March 1826 Anton's mother Gertrud Kirner, now twenty-nine, married Lorenz Hepting a clockmaker.

After the marriage, Anton, aged six, was shown for the first time as Anton Hepting and Lorenz shown as his father.

The reason this book has started with Anton's mother Gertrud rather than the father of Anton is because Gertrudis and Anton were born illegitimately and we cannot be absolutely sure that Lorenz Hepting was the biological father. It is probable that he was the father of both Gertrudis and Anton but was unable to marry Gertrud due to the marriage legislation at that time. It may have taken Lorenz several years to save enough money and to prove to the authorities that he could provide for his wife Gertrud and Anton once married. With proof of his status the authorities would have granted permission for the marriage to go ahead. The question raised by Jim Hepting was that if Lorenz was the father it would be expected that his name would have appeared on the birth record. This omission may have been to protect him from the authorities, or, unless a couple were married perhaps the father could not be registered as such. We can only be sure that our male blood line starts with Anton – possibly Lorenz's son.

The surname of Hepting may only be ours by marriage and as Jim Hepting said, we are definitely descended from Gertrud Kirner, so perhaps our surname should have been Kirner!

According to German legitimacy law at the time, if an unmarried couple have a child and subsequently marry, the child is automatically legitimised on that marriage and takes his father's surname. I think this is what happened in the case of Anton.

Jim employed the services of a German genealogist to locate any papers relating to Anton. Whilst he found Anton's original birth record and the marriage record of

Gertrud and Lorenz, he found no adoption papers.

The marriage prevention legislation, the legitimacy law and the fact that no adoption papers were found would seem to suggest that Lorenz was the biological father of Anton and is our legitimate ancestor. I have noted the parents of Lorenz Hepting in this book so that they can be followed back in time, if required.

Lorenz Hepting and Gertrud Kirner were married on 24th March 1826, almost seven years after the birth of Anton and nine years after the birth of Gertrudis.

There were differing views and debates among his descendants about the delay of the marriage. Sidney Robert Hepting believed that Lorenz was the father and that for some reason they couldn't marry for the first six years of Anton's life. Bill Hepting thought the same but couldn't understand why he wasn't named on the birth record if that was the case. However, Jim, their brother, was still doubtful that Lorenz was the father on the same basis that the birth record did not name Lorenz as the father and therefore he was unlikely to be so.

Jim and I discussed this information regarding the marriage prevention legislation and legitimacy laws but this didn't completely convince Jim that Lorenz was most likely the biological father of Anton. His reasoning was that it was traditional for the first son to be named after the father and clearly Anton wasn't. This may have been a deliberate deception on the part of Gertrud in order to protect Lorenz, as those who went ahead and had children before they married were fined and publicly humiliated. Despite this, illegitimate births were a frequent occurrence as most people could not afford to get married.

The parents of illegitimate children were subjected to a demeaning interrogation by the village judges and fined (the maximum allowable fine was 12 florin). A worse fate, for some, was to be exposed publicly in front of the congregation in church. The woman with a straw garland on her head, the man with a straw sword at his side.

Interestingly, more than thirty-five years after we started this research there is now a transcribed record showing Lorenz Hepting as father of Anton on his christening record. The christening record is shown on the transcribed records by the members of the Church of the Latter Day Saints and can be seen on the Family Search website. This record doesn't appear to have been found by the genealogist that Jim employed. A transcription of Anton's original birth record is shown later in this book, supplied by Jim Hepting.

If Lorenz was not the father, who was? You will have to make up your own minds, 'who do you think you are?'

Either way, Gertrud could have had no idea just how many lives would come into being from the birth of Anton in successive generations of the Hepting family stretching forward in time. Without Gertrud and the birth of illegitimate Anton, none of us would be here!

I have been unable to locate a date of death for Gertrud (Kirner) Hepting.

Gertrud's mother, Justina, born in 1760, died in April 1822 aged sixty-two. This was six months before daughter Helena married. During 1819-1824 a cholera pandemic raged across the European and Asian continents in which more than 100,000 people died and this may have been the cause of Justina's death.

Joseph, Gertrud's father, was born in 1759 and was buried on 14th March 1835, aged seventy-six.

Lorenz HEPTING

Lorenz Hepting was born in Hosskirch, a small village approximately 62 miles (100km) east of Eisenbach in the Black Forest. Lorenz was born in August 1790 to parents Aloysius Hepting born 1761 and Maria (Willman) Hepting born in 1750. They were married on 4th May 1784 in Friedenweiler.

Lorenz and Gertrud may have met through her father as both Lorenz and Joseph Kirner were clockmakers. Lorenz was thirty-six when he married Gertrud Kirner in 1826. I have not found any record of children born to Gertrud and Lorenz after their marriage. This may also lend credence to the belief that Lorenz was the father of both Gertrudis and Anton. It is believed that they lived in Eisenbach after their marriage.

Lorenz died in the village of Eisenbach and was buried on 16th March 1859 aged sixty-eight. Shown below are the reference details of the probate record available for Lorenz Hepting from the German Landesarchives.

Department of Justice, District courts
Order signature: G 550/1 No. 4649
Archival identifier: 5-2227937
Permalink:http://www.landesarchiv-bw.de/plink/?f=5-2227937
Title: Probate: Hepting, Lorenz, watchmakers, Eisenbach
Date: 1859
Circumference: 6 bl Pre-signatures: B 29 / 4_F_127; GLA 281/763

Anton KIRNER (HEPTING after 1826)

Anton was born to Gertrud Kirner in the same year that Queen Victoria and her husband Prince Albert of Saxe-Coburg and Gotha were born, 1819. Anton's birth and life however were a little different!

Anton was born at 12.30am on 3rd June in the village of Eisenbach in the Black Forest of southern Germany. The birth record shows that he was born to single mother Gertrud, aged twenty-two.

We know little of Anton's life as a child but he would have been educated and most likely have been taught the art of carving and clock making by his father and grandfather. We do know from later records that he became a successful clockmaker and lived at Hintergass in Eisenbach.

Anton would have been raised by Gertrud, perhaps with the help of her parents Justina and Joseph and her sisters. Lorenz, probably his father, may have lived with Gertrud and the family until they married.

Anton may have attended a local school or possibly been taught at home. Education was considered very important and children were well educated in this region even in the early 1800's.

Most houses would have had some land attached to enable produce to be grown and to keep small animals such as pigs and chickens to provide food for the family. Any surplus could be taken to market in Freiberg to sell. Some kept their animals in a hay loft attached to the house. It's not known if our ancestors had any farmland or if their whole way of life was clockmaking by this time.

It is well documented that clockmaking, carving and furniture making etc. in this region only grew out of the need for farmers to have another skill in the winter months, whilst unable to grow crops. This would have given them a small income to live on through those colder months. It's probable then that the Hepting and Kirner families did have some small farming livelihood. Over time as their clockmaking businesses became more successful they may have given up on their farming life or perhaps passed it on to other members of the family to maintain. Anton, as a young boy, may have helped to look after the animals and to grow food in the summer and learned the craft of clockmaking in the winter months. We do know from later records that he only made his living as a clock and watch maker.

Common winter trades for farmers of the area were carpentry, wood carving, furniture making, clock face and case painting, lace making and other crafts that could bring in some money during the winter months when the farms could not produce crops. The wives and daughters would have collected fallen branches and twigs, some to burn on the open fires and other larger ones would have been stored for some time to dry out and then used for carpentry and carving to make furniture, clock cases and internal movements for the clocks. There was after all plenty of wood in the Black Forest.

On 16th October 1843, when Anton Hepting was twenty-four years old he married Maria Ganter, aged twenty-five. Their marriage was registered in Friedenweiler. Maria was born on 14th December 1817 to parents Johanis Ganter and Magdelena Beha. They married in 1815. The Ganter family lived in Ebenemooshof, Eisenbach. Records show that Anton was doing very well in his business and sold many clocks and parts to various customers and businesses in Eisenbach and the surrounding villages. This may have allowed him to marry at what was then quite a young age. In his later career, from 1857 onwards, he settled down to provide clocks and clock parts to just one clockmaker and dealer, Johannes Baptista Beha and so had a very secure income for the rest of his working life.

In 1867 Springmann, a clockmaker who made many of the spring-loaded clocks in the area and worked as a homeworker for Johannes Baptista Beha, passed away. Most clockmakers worked from their homes at this time. Anton Hepting then took over some of his work but was unable to take it all over as he didn't have the necessary skills to produce the spring loaded mechanism. Although Anton was born and lived most of his life in Eisenbach, in his earlier career he lived in Friedenweiler for a time. This may have been where he met his wife Maria Ganter as he was working for Johanis Ganter (also recorded as Ivo in some records), Maria's father.

In 1873 Anton had an income of 1,729 guilders, as shown in the extracts of Anton's account book. This was a very good income at that time. Not all years were as good but working solely for Beha meant that he had a regular income. The account book ends in 1890 when Anton was seventy-one years of age and it's clear that his handwriting is beginning to show that perhaps his hands weren't as steady as they once were. In earlier years his writing showed a steady hand with enthusiastic flourishes, perhaps indicating someone who was very confident, happy with his lot and proud of what he had achieved in his life.

Johannes Baptista Beha was a very successful clock and watchmaker and dealer and exported clocks around the world, including to the UK, Russia and India. More information can be found on Johannes Baptista Beha on a Wikipedia webpage, the address is shown in the Resource and Further Reference section of this book.

Gunter Hepting, a descendant of Anton and distant relative who lives in Germany shared a copy of an article about Anton's life, including a copy of his account book from that time. Some descendants still live in Eisenbach and the surrounding villages. The article was written after records belonging to Anton were found when the house in which he had lived in Eisenbach was cleared in the year 2000. Gunter is a descendant of Anton and Maria's son, Bernhard Hepting.

According to the article, written from the records recovered from Anton's house, Anton and Maria had eight children including two that had died. However I have only found seven children including one that died. There may therefore be one child missing from my records. Anton and Maria's seven children for whom I have found records, were Justina, Sophia, Anton (later referred to as Anthony), Bernhard, Maria, Markus and Alois.

Anton's wife Maria died on 24th July 1883, aged sixty-five.

Anton was a founding member and advisor of the Eisenbach Trade Association, founded in 1883.

Anton continued working until 1890 a couple of years before his death on 26th July 1892 in Eisenbach aged seventy-three. His son in law Joseph Jaeggle was appointed executor of his will.

Anton's house in Hintergass, Eisenbach

The picture below shows Anton's house on Hintergass in Eisenbach. According to records he was known as 'Gasse Anton' because of where he lived. The house is set close to the steep wooded slopes that rise above the village. I believe that the house shown was the one cleared in the year 2000 where documents were found regarding Anton's life.

Extract copies of Anton Hepting's income record book

		Jos Raff in Kappel [?]	Gut haben	Zahlung mit
1893 [?] August 9	6	[illegible] 11.48	10 48	zahlt 10 48
Sept 5	6	Magnus Vogt [?] Eisenbach [?] [illegible] 2	12	zahlt 12
Nov 2	6	Paul Gander [?] Rudenberg [?] [illegible] à 1.6	6 36	zahlt 6 36
do 5	6	Jos Heitzmann [?] Eisenbach [?] [illegible] à 2	12	zahlt 12
do 5	2	Paul Gander [?] Rudenberg [?] [illegible] 2	4	zahlt 4
Dezbr 24	6	Burger [?] in [illegible] [illegible] 2.36	15 36	zahlt 15 36
do 24	12	[illegible] in Neustadt [?] [illegible]	10	zahlt 10
		[illegible]	71 .0	71

1849

10

Zusammenstellung

Nummer	Stück		Nummer		
65	80		65	121	24
66	126		66	169	16
67	82		67	161	12
68	60		68	107	24
69	150		69	247	–
Summa	355	Summa	f.	566	16
		[illegible]		16	
			f.	522	16

Rückständige von 1856

Johan Hofmann [illegible]	11	36	zalt	11 36
Alois Kramer [illegible]	29	12	zalt	29 12
Fidel [illegible]	12	–	zalt	12 –
Lodegar Brugger [illegible]	21	36	zalt	21 36
Magnus Koch	12	–	zalt	12 –

1856

Rechnung für Jahr 1873

Zusammenstellung

für

Anton [illegible]

		fl.	kr.
Jänner	[illegible]	161	6
Februar	[illegible]	148	15
März	[illegible]	149	42
April	[illegible]	151	49
Mai	[illegible]	125	8
Juni	[illegible]	130	12
Juli	[illegible]	122	29
August	[illegible]	132	30
September	[illegible]	157	54
Oktober	[illegible]	145	57
November	[illegible]	149	22
Dezember	[illegible]	115	2
	Zusammen	1729	29

Anton [illegible]

1873

Die letzte Seite des Kontobuchs 1890.

A copy of Anton's original birth record

Im jahr 1819 den 3 juni nacht halb 12 uhr ist zu Eisenbach geborhren und am 4 juni fruh um 8 uhr von Vikar Schadler getauft worden Anton unehelicher Sohn der ledigen Gertrud Kirner von Eisenbach. Tauf zeugen waren: Thadda Kirner und Gertrud Heitzman burgh von Eisenbach auch jos. A Messner.

Translation of the above record

In the year 1819, at night on the 3rd of June at half past twelve, he was born in Eisenbach and on the 4th of June at 8:00 am he was baptized by Vicar Schadler, Anton, the illegitimate son of the unmarried Gertrud Kirner of Eisenbach. Baptism witnesses were: Thadda Kirner and Gertrud Heitzman citizen of Eisenbach also jos. A Messner.

Children of Anton and Maria HEPTING

The article previously mentioned stated that Anton and Maria had eight children including two that had died. The details of the seven children that I have located in the records, including one that died young, follow. I have also shown the grandchildren of Anton and Maria for which I have been able to find records.

Justina was born on 10th September 1844 and married Joseph Jaeggle on 8th February 1877. Joseph was born in 1846 to parents Magnus Jaeggle and Maria Lagenbach. Joseph was a clockmaker and mayor of Eisenbach.

Justina and Joseph Jaeggle had three children, Bernhard born on 3rd August 1878, Johanna on 1st April 1880 and Justina on 11th June 1885.

Sophia was born on 10th May 1846 but sadly died on 17th June 1849, just three years of age.

Anton was born 6th January 1849 and anglicised his name to Anthony after emigrating to England in 1867. On 3rd July 1872 in London, Anthony married Louisa Ann Hack. We follow Anthony in part two.

Bernhard was born on 20th July 1851 and married Maria Tritschler on 17th January 1878. Maria was born in 1853 to parents Joseph Tritschler and Maria Beha. Bernhard also became a clockmaker and produced clocks and parts for Winterhalder and Hoffmeier in Neustadt, a local town.

Bernhard and Maria had six children, Maria born on 31st July 1878, Anna on 15th July 1881, Karolina on

12th August 1885, Leopold on 7th October 1888, Ida on 27th July 1891 and Bernhard on 16th August 1894.

Gunter Hepting's parents gave him a photo of the descendants of Bernhard Hepting and he kindly sent that photo to me. The photo was taken during the second world war. Those of you who knew Raymond Hepting, will see the similarity between Raymond and Alfons in the photo at the end of this section.

Gunter also sent the picture of Anton's house in Eisenbach, shown previously.

Maria was born on 8th August 1853 and married Karl Spitz on 8th November 1881. Karl was born in 1851 to parents Kaspar Spitz and Maria Wehrle

Maria and Karl had seven children. Friedrich, the first child was born and died on 5th March 1883, Maria Wilhelmine was born on 23rd March 1884, Juditha on 15th August 1885, Franciscus on 21st September 1886, Karolina on 16th October 1888, Amanda was born on 24th February 1890 and died on 21st August 1890 at six months of age and Anna was born on 19th June 1893.

Markus was born in Eisenbach on 8th February 1855. Markus emigrated to England in 1872 to take up an apprenticeship in watch and clockmaking in London. A little of Markus' life is shown in subsequent pages.

Alois was born on 12th June 1858 and married Ludwina Hettich on 20th November 1888. Ludwina was born in 1866 to Theodor Hettich and Barbara Kleiser

Alois and Ludwina had four children. Andreas was born on 15th February 1887, he was born before Alois and Ludwina married, the records do not name Alois as father but it may have been a similar situation to Gertrud and Lorenz. Johannes was born on 23rd June 1891, Antonius was born on 19th April 1893 and sadly died on 23rd December 1893 and Albert was born on 1st August 1895.

I have not researched the lives of Anton's (Anthony's) brothers and sisters going forward, other than that shown on the previous pages.

However, as Markus also came to London, some research was carried out and I have since added to that and show a little more of Markus' life after he emigrated to England, in part two.

Descendants of Bernhard Hepting born in 1851
Alfons – top left

This photo was taken during the second world war

Part Two

Hepting

A Family History

England

1867 – 2020

Anton (Anthony) and Louisa (Hack) Hepting Family Tree – England

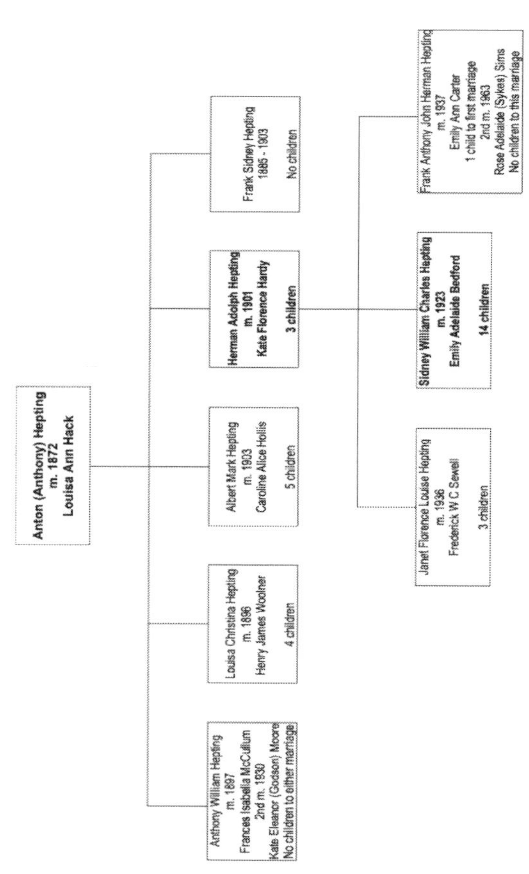
Anton (Anthony) Hepting
m. 1872
Louisa Ann Hack
Anthony William Hepting
m. 1897
Frances Isabella McCullum
2nd m. 1930
Kate Eleanor (Godson) Moore
No children to either marriage
Louisa Christina Hepting
m. 1896
Henry James Woolner
4 children
Albert Mark Hepting
m. 1903
Caroline Alice Hollis
5 children
Herman Adolph Hepting
m. 1901
Kate Florence Hardy
3 children
Frank Sidney Hepting
1885 - 1903
No children
Janet Florence Louise Hepting
m. 1936
Frederick W C Sewell
3 children
Sidney William Charles Hepting
m. 1923
Emily Adelaide Bedford
14 children
Frank Anthony John Herman Hepting
m. 1937
Emily Ann Carter
1 child to first marriage
2nd m. 1963
Rose Adelaide (Sykes) Sims
No children to this marriage

The Hepting Family Tree – England

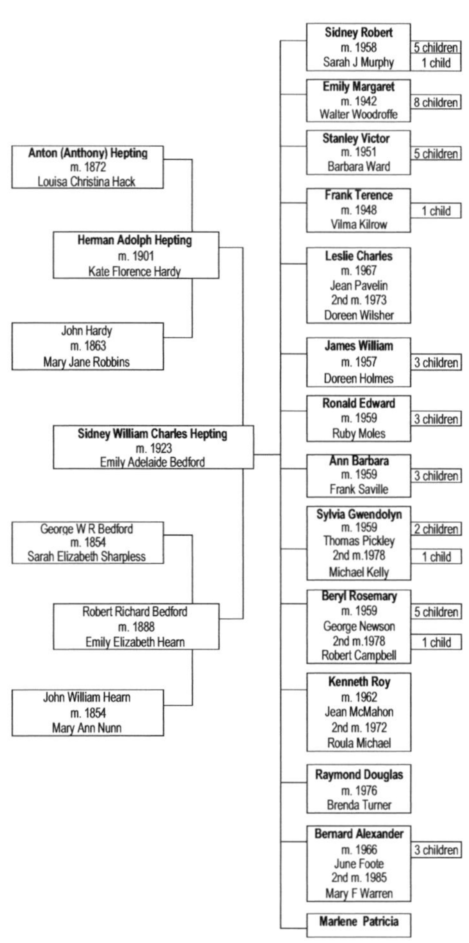

Anton (Anthony) Hepting
m. 1872
Louisa Christina Hack
Herman Adolph Hepting
m. 1901
Kate Florence Hardy
John Hardy
m. 1863
Mary Jane Robbins
Sidney William Charles Hepting
m. 1923
Emily Adelaide Bedford
George W R Bedford
m. 1854
Sarah Elizabeth Sharpless
Robert Richard Bedford
m. 1888
Emily Elizabeth Hearn
John William Hearn
m. 1854
Mary Ann Nunn
Sidney Robert
m. 1958
Sarah J Murphy
5 children
1 child
Emily Margaret
m. 1942
Walter Woodroffe
8 children
Stanley Victor
m. 1951
Barbara Ward
5 children
Frank Terence
m. 1948
Vilma Kilrow
1 child
Leslie Charles
m. 1967
Jean Pavelin
2nd m. 1973
Doreen Wilsher
James William
m. 1957
Doreen Holmes
3 children
Ronald Edward
m. 1959
Ruby Moles
3 children
Ann Barbara
m. 1959
Frank Saville
3 children
Sylvia Gwendolyn
m. 1959
Thomas Pickley
2nd m.1978
Michael Kelly
2 children
1 child
Beryl Rosemary
m. 1959
George Newson
2nd m.1978
Robert Campbell
5 children
1 child
Kenneth Roy
m. 1962
Jean McMahon
2nd m. 1972
Roula Michael
Raymond Douglas
m. 1976
Brenda Turner
Bernard Alexander
m. 1966
June Foote
2nd m. 1985
Mary F Warren
3 children
Marlene Patricia

Markus

Son of Anton and Maria HEPTING

Markus Hepting was born in Eisenbach on 8th February 1855. He emigrated to England, arriving in London in 1872, although not in time to see his brother Anton (Anthony) marry Louisa Ann Hack in July 1872. It may have been Markus' intention to be here for their marriage but perhaps his travel papers were delayed and he was unable to get here for their July wedding.

Markus was also an apprentice watch and clock maker and no doubt came to London to further his career. I cannot find any record of Markus between his arrival in 1872 and 1881. However in 1881 he is living at 38 Blackman Street, Lambeth, London and was recorded as a 'servant' clock and watchmaker for a family of clock and watchmakers called Straub. It is believed that this is where he served his apprenticeship when he first arrived in 1872.

Listed as the head of the household on the 1881 census was widower Katherina Straub, aged thirty-five, she was born in Neustadt in Germany and so she may have been known to Markus' father, Anton. Katherina was running the business that had no doubt been established by her husband before he died. She had five children under the age of nine. Her husband had died the previous year in 1880. There were also several clock and watchmaker workers living and working at the address. The clock and watchmakers were our Markus Hepting, Adolph Ganter and Joseph Tritschler. I don't know if Ganter and Tritschler from Germany were related to Markus through marriages but each of these surnames do appear in our own family history and so it's most likely that they were relations, even if distant ones, and that they knew each other well. Markus was just seventeen years of age when he arrived in London.

On the 1881 census Markus' name is shown as Hebting. This is a common misspelling as the name can easily be misunderstood in speech. I'm sure that all those with the surname of Hepting have had to spell their name almost every time they've said it, I know I did!

I can find no further record of Markus until he appears on an electoral roll in 1893 at 4 Hinton Terrace, Norwood. Markus is shown on the electoral roll each year at this address until 1898.

On the 1901 census Markus was living and working at 8a The Broadway, Islington where he was running his own business in rented premises. The building of this new parade of shops was completed in 1895 (I understand that 'The Broadway' changed its name to 'The Parade' in 1908). Markus was a clock and watchmaker but would have sold other jewellery items in his shop too. Markus is believed to have had an irritating skin condition which caused him some distress, this may have been psoriasis or other skin ailment.

According to a newspaper report, on a Monday morning in November of 1901 the estate agent who had let the shop to Markus went to call on him for some back rent. The shop wasn't open that morning when he arrived and so the estate agent knocked on the door, getting no answer he went back to his office.

Later that day he called on Markus again but the shop remained closed. The estate agent became suspicious and called on the police to enter the property.

Markus was found on the bed, in the back parlour of the shop where he lived, having committed suicide by cutting his own throat through the windpipe with his razor. This lay on the bed beside his body.

Markus never married, he was aged just forty-six when he died in November 1901.

When his brother Anton (Anthony) was informed he said that he had seen Markus a fortnight before and he had seemed in good spirits apart from stating that his business was a little slow.

In the newspaper article, from which this information was taken, it stated that Louisa Davison had said that she had seen Markus recently and had advised him to go to a medical man as he appeared depressed.

There is no mention of who Louisa Davison was or how she knew Markus.

The coroner's report stated that Markus had committed suicide by his own hand while of unsound mind.

Anton (Anthony)

Son of Anton and Maria HEPTING

Anton (later known as Anthony). To save any confusion with his father I will refer to Anton as Anthony from here on. Anthony was born 6th January 1849 and grew up in Eisenbach in the Black Forest area of Germany. Anthony's father would no doubt have taught his son how to make clocks and watches when he was young. When Anthony emigrated to London in 1867 he was just eighteen years of age. Before he was able to leave he had to apply to the Grand Duke, the ruler of that nation state of Germany, for permission to leave and for travel papers.

Anthony's father was doing very well in his business and documents held in the German archives show that he was able to pay for all Anthony's travel, apprenticeship costs and expenses to give him the opportunity of a better life for himself in London.

Apprentices rarely received any pay for the work they did. This was still the case in the middle 1900's in England. It was common for the apprentice or his family to pay the business owner for the apprenticeship and the payment would normally include lodgings at the business premises and day to day expenses.

It was the practice in the Black Forest during the 1800's for the family to save enough money for the eldest son to find work elsewhere. Often the son would go to live with family or friends of the family already living abroad or to live in the business premises where their apprenticeship would be carried on. Unlike in England, at that time, it was usual for the youngest son to inherit the house, farm or whatever assets remained on the death of the father. The eldest son could remain and work for his younger brother or find a life elsewhere. This was to ensure that ownership of the assets remained within the family for the longest possible time than may have been the case if the inheritance went to the eldest son.

London, during the 1800's and its siting on the River Thames, was a very busy major trading port and because of the increasingly large population would have provided many opportunities for selling the clocks and watches that Anthony made. This would have afforded him the ability to make himself a wealthy man at that time.

Whether Anthony and others like him who emigrated had any intention of returning home once they had completed their apprenticeships and had made their way in life we don't know. A few did return to their homeland but most remained in their new home.

When Anthony arrived in London in 1867, Queen Victoria was on the throne and in mourning for her husband, Prince Albert, who had died six years earlier. Also in that year, the first foundation stone was laid for the Royal Albert Hall.

London in the 1860's would have been a very different place to that of Anthony's home village of Eisenbach. The air in Eisenbach would have been clean and fresh and there would have been fresh mountain water to drink. Little has changed in the landscape and what you see today is very much what Anthony would have seen when he left his home there.

In London he would have found the opposite. No fresh drinking water, overcrowded houses and filthy streets, shared toilet facilities, bad smelling air and very crowded and dangerous roads with little or no traffic control. Anthony must have wondered what he'd come to and why he didn't want to return immediately I cannot imagine! Learning his trade and not wanting to let his parents down and the instability of his homeland, no doubt drove him onward.

It must have been quite a shock for Anthony when he arrived though. London was very busy with horse drawn carts and carriages jamming the roads and the attendant horse waste on the streets. There were areas of great poverty across London with many families sharing houses and toilets with little or no sanitation. In many London streets there would only be one or two toilets for the whole of the street and one drinking water standpipe or well from which the water for the street was drawn.

There were many workhouses around London at that time and some families were so poor that they had to give up their new-born children to the workhouse as they couldn't afford to feed them. Many children would not have had shoes and would have walked barefoot on the cobbles of the dirty streets. Large numbers of babies and children died throughout the 1800's and life expectancy generally was very low. Very young children, some as young as five, who came from impoverished families would have worked, either as chimney sweeps assistants or flower girls and those a bit older, in the match factories, this work was dangerous and hazardous to their health. Things improved when schooling became more widespread and free.

There were some nice green parks which may have reminded Anthony of his home. Records show that at this time and certainly from 1754 there were already people with the surname of Hepting living in England.

They were possibly relatives but I have not linked them to Anthony to date. Most of those living in London were clock and watchmakers and Anthony may have known them.

In December 1868 we know that Anthony was not settling down well in London. He wrote a letter to his parents, stating that he didn't like where he was and his business was not doing well and he hoped it would do better in America. He asked his parents to apply to the Grand Duke for permission to go to America. As a subject of the Baden region and of the Grand Duke, permission had to be sought for movement anywhere including between countries outside of the nation states. The awful conditions in London wouldn't have helped either and he may not have been well treated in his apprenticeship or was lonely. It may have been a combination of these factors that made him want to go to America.

At the end of this section there are transcriptions and translations of Anthony's letter to his parents and the application to the Duke for permission for Anthony to travel to America.

Whether his parents advised him against going to America, possibly permission wasn't granted for him to travel or for some other reason, Anthony decided to stay. He stayed and our Hepting line flourished. But for this change of heart or denial for Anthony to travel, we, as Jim Hepting said, could all have been American.

In 1871 Anthony was living as a lodger in the house of a George and Mary Bowman at 3 Little Marylebone Street, London and was trading as a watchmaker.

It was common practice for many unrelated families to live in the same house, using the same front door but renting a number of rooms. Depending on the size of the house, each family may rent one, two or more rooms and in the better areas and houses there would have been an outside toilet which would have been shared with all the families in that house. Only in the bigger, grander houses and palaces would there have been bathrooms.

Perhaps by 1871 Anthony's business had improved, or he had already met Louisa, his wife to be, as all efforts to go to America seem to have ceased. On the 3rd July 1872 Anthony married Louisa Ann Hack in the Parish Church of St. Marylebone in London.

Louisa was born in London in September 1851. Her father, although shown as Henry Hack on the marriage certificate, was born Heinrich Karl Ludwig Hack in Germany and was a tailor. Her mother, Mary Ann Binstead, was born in 1833 in Brixham in Devon and her father was a servant. When Louisa was ten years old the Hack family were living at 10 Little Portland Street, St. Marylebone.

After their marriage, Anthony and Louisa moved to 6 Winsley Street in London. Ten years later in 1881 they had moved to 37 Newman Street in London. In the nine years following their marriage they had three children, Anthony William born in 1873, Louisa Christina born in 1875 and Albert Mark born in 1876. The cost of the two unfurnished rooms that Anthony and Louisa rented on the first floor of 37 Newman Street in 1881 was eleven shillings per week (fifty-five pence for the younger among us and in terms of its value in 2021 it would be approximately seventy pounds).

By 1891 Anthony and Louisa had two more children, Herman Adolph born in 1881 and Frank Sidney born in 1885. The family were still living at 37 Newman Street and it must have been getting very crowded as there were now five children in just two rooms. Their eldest child, Anthony William aged seventeen, was a surgical instrument maker's apprentice. Louisa Christina aged sixteen was a milliner's assistant and Albert Mark aged fourteen was an apprentice watch and clockmaker, following in his father's footsteps. Herman Adolph and Frank Sidney were at school aged nine and five respectively.

In 1901 Anthony and Louisa are still at 37 Newman Street but now with only three of their children living at home. Albert, now aged twenty-four, is a private in the British Army. Herman, aged nineteen, is a French Polisher and Frank, aged fifteen, is a hairdresser. Louisa Christina had married in 1896 and Anthony William was married the following year in 1897.

In late 1901 news came that Anthony's brother Markus had been found dead at his shop. This must have been difficult for Anthony as Markus was the only one of his birth family to join him in England.

Just two years later in 1903, Anthony and Louisa's son Frank Sidney died, aged eighteen. Records state that he died from a burst appendix and cardiac arrest.

Four years later in 1907, Anthony aged fifty-eight, husband of Louisa and father to their five children was admitted under the lunacy patient admissions to the London County Lunatic Asylum Hanwell, Norwood, Middlesex. Because of data privacy the 'reason for infirmity' column has been redacted. Anthony may have been suffering from depression or dementia or other medical condition not completely understood at that time.

It was known in the family that he would suffer bouts of anger, had a foul temper and would strike out at his wife Louisa. According to his granddaughter Louisa Frances, daughter of Albert Mark, Anthony used to visit the clubs in Soho, come home drunk and get violent. His granddaughter Louisa said that she clashed with Anthony many times over how he treated her grandmother. The drinking and violence had become so bad that his wife Louisa would hide his boots so that he couldn't go out and get drunk. This led to him very nearly strangling his wife in a fit of rage. This was perhaps the last straw for his wife Louisa and may have been the reason for him being admitted to the asylum.

It's unknown what condition Anthony was suffering from but in the early part of the 1900's mental health was not fully understood or treated in the same way as it would be today. Anthony's brother Markus had died in 1901, his son Frank had also died in 1903 and so it's possible that he was suffering from depression or Alzheimer's. Whatever the cause, Anthony lived out the rest of his life as a patient of Hanwell asylum until his death on 17th April 1920 aged seventy-one, he had spent thirteen years there.

During this time I wonder if he would have been aware of the war between his homeland of Germany and his adopted country or of the deaths in the family during that time. Was he aware of the Spanish flu pandemic that took hold after the war in the years 1918-1920 killing over fifty million people worldwide. It's not known if Anthony was aware of any of this, or because of his condition, he was oblivious to it all. It would not have been a very pleasant existence for him as patients were not always treated very well. It's not known if any of his family visited him at the hospital or if he even knew that his wife Louisa had died in 1916.

On his death in 1920 his daughter Louisa Christina registered his death and arranged for him to be buried in Tottenham Cemetery in North London, near to her home.

Anthony's wife Louisa had remained in London until after the 1911 census which sees her living on her own at 19 Great Chapel Street, just off Oxford Street in London. The remaining children had married and moved to homes of their own.

Sometime between May 1911 and 1916 Louisa Ann went to live with her daughter Louisa Christina and her husband Henry Woolner, in Edmonton, North London.

Louisa Ann passed away in March 1916, aged sixty-four.

The following letter was sent from Anthony to his parents in the Black Forest in December 1868. This was kindly translated by a German lady from a copy obtained from the German archives by Jim Hepting.

A translation of Anthony's original letter

London 6th Dec 1868

Very Dear Parents

I beg you to help me. I hope you will be so good because I want to emigrate to America, if you would be so good to enquire for me to get the necessary papers. I need them from the authorities, The Grand Duchy, who will issue them for you. I want to go because I like not where I am now because my business is very bad and I believe to do much better business over there.

I hope you don't mind that I ask you to help me. News, I don't have anything to write. I am healthy and hope the same from you as well.

I give my love to father, mother and brothers and sisters.

Your thankful son

Anton Hepting

The following extract is also a copy, obtained by Jim Hepting from the German archives, of the passport application document given to the Grand Duchy district office requesting permission for Anton (Anthony) to go to America. The document translation is below.

A copy of Anton's (Anthony) passport application

Anton Hepting, von hier gebohren am 6 Janner 1849 und ist im Jahr 1867 mit einem erthilten reisepass nach England, sich in der Taschen uhrmacherei and Uhrenhandel auszubilden. Jetzt wunscht derselbe sich nach Amerika zu begeben. Das grossherzogliche bezirksamt wird ersucht dem ledigen Anton Hepting gefalligst die Auswanderungserlaubnis ertheilen. Sein Vater Anton Hepting Burger von hier, macht sich fur ihn fur alle Kosten and Schulden verbundlich, ist auch zahlungsfahig.

Translation

Born from here on January 6th, 1849, in 1867, with a passport issued to England, he trained in pocket watchmaking and watch trade. Now he wishes to go to America. The grand-ducal district office is requested to grant the unmarried Anton Hepting the emigration permit. His father, Anton Hepting citizen of here, is responsible for all costs and debts, and is also able to pay.

Anthony William

Son of Anthony and Louisa HEPTING

Anthony William Hepting, the eldest child of Anthony and Louisa, was born in April 1873 and christened on 1st June 1873 at All Souls Church in the Parish of St. Marylebone, London. The family were living at 6 Winsley Street, London at the time of Anthony's birth.

In 1891 Anthony's profession is shown as a surgical instrument maker's apprentice. The family are now living at 37 Newman Street, London.

When Anthony was twenty-four he married Frances (Fanny) Isabella McCullum on 2nd October 1897 in St. Andrews Church, Wells Street, St. Marylebone. On the marriage certificate they both give their address as 37 Newman Street and so it's possible that the two families each rented rooms in this building or that the address was given to enable them to marry at that church. Often the church would insist that the couple to be married were parishioners.

Fanny was born in 1873 in Chatham, Kent. Later records suggest 1875 but dates do not always match perfectly, even in official records. Until the 1911 census all records were completed by an enumerator who took details of those living at each address. If the occupiers were out at the time, neighbours may have given incorrect information to the enumerator.

It seems that Fanny moved to London between 1891 and 1897. Whether she went on her own or with her family is not known. Her father had died in 1890 when the family were still living in Chatham. I have not been able to find any records of the McCullum family living in London.

In 1901 Anthony and Fanny had moved to 120 Great Titchfield Street, St. Marylebone, London. By 1911 they had moved to 24 Sebright Road, Barnet, Hertfordshire. There were no children shown on this census. Anthony by this time was now shown as a dental instrument and false teeth maker.

In 1925 they were living at 3 Alston Road, Barnet. Four years later in April 1929 Fanny died aged fifty-six.

Anthony remained in the same house and the following year in October 1930 he married Kate Eleanor (Godson) Moore. Kate was born on 14th November 1863 in Mansfield, Nottingham. Kate was first married to Rupert Moore in 1882 and the family lived in Nottingham but later moved to Barnet. Rupert passed away in 1926. Their marriage had produced two daughters and one son.

Sometime in the following nine years Anthony William and Kate Eleanor had moved to 62 Wentworth Road in Barnet.

Kate passed away early in 1940 aged seventy-seven.

After Kate's death Anthony moved to Woodhouse Farm in Branscombe, Devon, probably to be closer to, Florence Gertrude, Kate's daughter from her previous marriage to Rupert, who lived in Branscombe.

Anthony William passed away on 2nd February 1943, aged seventy. He was buried in Branscombe. On his death he left his estate to his step daughter, Florence Gertrude (Moore) Butter.

Florence passed away in 1950 aged sixty-six, her address at the time was the Post Office, Bank Cottage, Branscombe in Devon.

Louisa Christina

Daughter of Anthony and Louisa HEPTING

Louisa Christina Hepting was born on 3rd January 1875 and christened on 7th February 1875 at All Souls Church in London. In 1891 she was a milliner's assistant, aged sixteen. *Jim Hepting remembers Louisa and sent me the following description of her.* ' Louisa was a large blonde woman with a long plait that reached down her back, was softly spoken and always smiling.'

In 1896, aged twenty-one, Louisa married Henry James Woolner who was born on 28th February 1873, he was a cabinet maker. The origins of Henry's family surname are in Suffolk.

In 1901 the family were living at 11 Stratford Place, St. Pancras, London. Henry and Louisa were shown on the census of that year but Harry, their first born son, who was three at the time, was with his grandparents on the day the census was taken. It's possible that he was just there for one night. Even if a person was only staying at an address for one night they had to be recorded at that address and not their usual address. This was to ensure that people were not included in the census records twice.

By 1911 the family had moved to 163 Northumberland Park in Tottenham, North London and now there were three children, Harry, Winifred Christine and Dorothy Rose. Their fourth child, Norman Frank was born in 1913.

In 1933 they'd moved again to another house in the same road, 200 Northumberland Park. Jim Hepting visited them on many occasions when he was a child and he and his brothers and sisters all knew Louisa as Auntie Lou, although she was their Great Aunt (their grandfather's sister). Jim said that whenever he visited Louisa she would give him a shilling to spend on himself and a ready, made up bag of sweets.

Louisa and Henry's life was blighted by two world wars, the first world war took the life of their first born son Harry, aged just nineteen. Louisa's mother died in March 1916 and her son in September 1916 and so it must have been a very sad time for the family.

During the second world war, in 1940, Louisa's husband Henry James Woolner passed away aged sixty-seven.

Shortly after Henry died Louisa went to live with her daughter Winifred and her husband, Frank.

Louisa lived another twenty-four years after Henry died, passing away aged eighty-nine on 30th October 1964. On her passing Louisa was living at a nursing home at 17 Upper Maze Hill, St. Leonards on Sea. Before going into the nursing home she was living with her daughter Winifred at 13 Maplehurst Road in St. Leonards on Sea. Louisa left her estate of £623 to her daughter Winifred in her will.

Children of Henry and Louisa WOOLNER

Harry Woolner, the first of Louisa and Henry's children, was born in 1897. Harry, once of age, joined up and became a Private in the British Army in the Duke of Cambridge's Own (Middlesex) Regiment, 1st 7th Battalion. His regiment number was T.F. 5394. Harry was posted to France and Flanders in world war one (1914-18).

Harry was wounded in Flanders and died from his

wounds on 14th September 1916, aged just nineteen. His loss must have been devastating to Louisa and Henry. To lose a son at such a young age whilst fighting in a war overseas would have been difficult enough but knowing that he was killed in a war fighting against his own grandfather's countrymen, must have been hard to bear. It would have been a difficult time for them all. Harry is buried in La Neuville British Cemetery at Corbie in France, plot 2D 39 headstone 689.

Winifred Christine Woolner was born on 24th December 1901 while the family were living at 11 Stratford Place, St. Pancras, London.

In 1939 Winifred was living at home with her parents in Edmonton, London and working as a railway clerk for London Transport.

In 1942 Winifred aged forty-one married Frank Hull Dyson. Frank was born on 23rd October 1888 in Holborn and was aged fifty-four when he married Winifred.

In 1911 when Frank was twenty-three he was a clerk at a printing works. During the first world war he was a rifleman in the British Army and received the Victory and the British War Medals.

Frank had previously married in 1916 to Ethel Amy Green but she had passed away in 1941. In 1939, although Frank was married to Ethel, she was not registered at the same address, it may be that she was in hospital or temporarily elsewhere and so couldn't be shown at her usual address. In 1939 Frank was living in Hackney and was a clerk for London County Council. Between 1962 and 1964 Frank and Winifred moved to Sussex. I have not found any record of children born to them.

Frank died, aged eighty-four, in the spring of 1973 in East Sussex.

Winifred was living at 13 Maplehurst Road, St. Leonards on Sea, East Sussex at the time of her death on 16th April 1994, aged ninety-two.

Dorothy Rose Woolner was born on 21st February 1906. She married Thomas Roland Dorcey in July 1937. Thomas was born on 17th July 1907 in Tottenham. On the 1939 Register Dorothy's occupation was shown as 'unpaid domestic duties', this was the term used for a housewife. Thomas was a local government officer in charge of costings, ledgers and stores accounts. They lived all their married lives at 117 Kenilworth Crescent, Enfield. Thomas's father, also called Thomas, came to live with them until his death in 1968.

Dorothy died a year before her father in law on 7th June 1967 aged sixty-one.

Thomas Roland Dorcey re-married in Haringey in 1969, two years after his wife Dorothy had passed away.

Thomas Roland died on 5th July 2001 aged ninety-three. Thomas Roland Dorcey's will shows that he bequeathed small sums to his second wife's two children. The bulk of his estate though was left to various charities. He had no children of his own from either marriage.

Norman Frank Woolner was born on 17th September 1913. Norman married Dorothy Hilda Harvey in the early part of 1938. Dorothy was born on 8th March 1916.

On the 1939 Register, they were living at 148 Lodge Avenue, Barking. Norman was a London County Council estate clerk and part time A.R.P. Warden and Dorothy was a shorthand typist.

In 1970 Norman and Dorothy were living at 36 Woodstock Gardens, Seven Kings, Ilford, Essex. They had two daughters, the first born in Bristol in late 1939 and the second born in Ilford in mid 1947.

The first daughter was born in Bristol but the family were living, at that time, in Barking. As the birth was towards the end of 1939 and at the start of the second world war it may have been that Dorothy, being pregnant, decided to go and stay in Bristol to avoid the onslaught of German bombers that was expected. The birth was registered to mother Dorothy Woolner with the maiden surname of Harvey, so this was the daughter of our Norman and Dorothy Woolner.

Norman died on 26th September 1970, aged fifty-seven.

Dorothy died on 11th April 2017, aged 101.

Dorothy's will does not mention the first daughter. At the time of making her will Dorothy was living in Romford, Essex. Her estate was left to her daughter, born in 1947. It's possible that the first daughter had passed away but I have not found a record to confirm this.

Albert Mark

Son of Anthony and Louisa HEPTING

Albert Mark Hepting was born on 28th July 1876. Albert, at the age of fourteen, was an apprentice clockmaker with his father. The hand-making of clocks and watches was by this time diminishing. Factories were manufacturing watches and clocks and the cost to the public was consequently reduced making their purchase more affordable compared to the hand-made ones. Albert changed direction to earn a living.

In 1897, Albert, aged twenty-one, joined up to serve in the British Army. He served initially for twelve years. Information recorded in the Army enlistment forms when Albert joined up shows that he was a slight man at five feet, three and three quarter inches, had a chest size of thirty-three inches, weighed one hundred and eighteen pounds (46.4 kg), had brown hair, a fair complexion, grey eyes and had a tattoo of a bunch of flowers on his left front forearm.

Albert was posted to fight in the Boer war in South Africa and was there from 1899 to 1901. He received the Queen's South Africa Medal for his service there.

In January 1903 Albert married Caroline Alice Hollis. Caroline was born in 1875. The family home was at 76 Whitfield Street in London.

In 1911, Albert's term with the army was complete and he was discharged. The family were still living at 76 Whitfield Street and Albert's occupation was shown as a house painter.

By the end of 1911 Albert and Caroline had five children, Louisa Frances, Albert, William Bernard, Dorothy and Harry.

In February 1915, Albert, now aged thirty-eight, enlisted again after the first world war broke out and was sent with the Expeditionary Force on 18th March 1915 to western France.

His role in the Army was recorded as Carman (driver). His unit was the RASC HT (Royal Army Service Corps Horse Transport). His duties as a Horse Transport driver would have involved moving men, artillery and supplies to the fighting line. Albert's nephew Harry, who was eighteen at the time, was also serving in France in the British Army.

By 1918 Albert had been promoted to Lance Corporal but in November of that same year he was caught smoking a cigarette in the forage barn and was punished for it. He was deprived of his Lance Corporal's stripe and reduced in rank to Private! Life and the rules were hard and the judgement swift.

Albert fortunately survived the war and was discharged from the Army on 27th May 1919. He had completed another four years after having signed up for the second time in 1915. Albert had served a total of just over sixteen years in the British Army and received various medals for his service during this war, the British Medal, the Victory Medal and the 1914-15 Star medal for his time in western France.

By 1920 Albert, Caroline and the family had moved to 14 Foley Street in London. Their first born son, according to tradition, was named Albert after his father.

Albert's wife Caroline died in January 1931 aged just fifty-five years.

In 1932 Albert Mark was living at 40 Howland Street, St. Pancras, London with three of his children, Louisa, William and Dorothy.

In 1939 Albert was living with his daughter Louisa Frances and son Harry in a flat at 10 Howard House, Cleveland Street, London. Both he and his son are recorded as general labourers.

Albert Mark died, aged sixty-three in June 1940.

Children of Albert and Caroline HEPTING

Louisa Frances Hepting was born 1st September 1903 and baptised on 23rd September 1903. The family lived at 37 Newman Street at the time of her birth. Louisa never married and remained at home. The family moved several times and by 1947 Louisa was living on her own at 10 Howard House, Cleveland Street, London. She later moved to Ingestre Court.

Louisa's cousins once removed, Sidney, Bill and Jim Hepting, visited her at her flat in Ingestre Court in London five years before she died. She told them that when she was much younger she had a gift shop in Oxford Street. She appeared in good health and didn't look her age. Louisa told them what she remembered of her father Albert Mark, her grandfather Anthony and of her uncle Herman.

Louisa Frances died aged ninety-eight in 2001.

Albert Hepting was born on 28th March 1905 at 76 Whitfield Street and died in November 1909 at just four years of age.

William Bernard Hepting was born on 6th February 1907 at 76 Whitfield Street. William married Lilian Rose Lucy Cartwright on 11th September 1932. Lilian was born on 9th April 1910. The marriage took place at Trinity Church, St. Marylebone in London.

Louisa Frances Hepting

Jim Hepting and Louisa Frances Hepting

William was twenty-five years old and living at 12 Upper Charlton Street West. His occupation was recorded as chauffeur. One of the witnesses at their marriage was George Baxter, he later married William's sister, Dorothy Winifred.

In 1933 they lived at 10 Clifton Road, Camden Square in London. By 1935 they had moved to 205 Stanhope Street and in 1939, William, his wife and their son Victor Bernard, were living at 29 Pemberton Terrace, Islington in London. William was now a van driver for the Bourne and Hollingsworth department store in London and an A.R.P. Warden (fireman). In 1953 the family were living at the same address as Lilian's parents, 13 Pemberton Terrace, Islington.

William died in April 1981 aged seventy-four.

Lilian died in 1995 aged eighty-five.

Victor Bernard

Grandson of Albert and Caroline HEPTING

Victor Bernard was born on 4th February 1934 to William Bernard and Lilian Rose Lucy (Cartwright) Hepting. Victor married June Letchford in 1957. June was born in 1938. In 1963 they were living at 13 Roseberry Road, London but by 1965 they had moved to Wood Green in North London. Victor and June had two children.

Victor died on 8th November 2002, aged sixty-eight.

Dorothy Winifred Hepting was born on 15th April 1909 and baptised at St. John the Evangelist church in Charlotte Street, Camden.

In December 1934, when Dorothy was twenty-five, she married George Baxter, aged twenty-four. George was born on 20th February 1910. He was a sheet metal worker and he lived at 35 Bolsover Street, Marylebone in London at the time of their marriage. They married at Trinity Church, Marylebone in London. Although Dorothy married George in 1934 she was shown on the electoral register as living with her father and siblings at 10 Howard House, Marylebone, as Dorothy Winifred Hepting, not Baxter, in 1935, 1936 and 1937. Dorothy is first shown as Dorothy Baxter in 1939 but still living with her father and siblings, five years after her marriage. In 1939 George was living at 21 Newmarket Road, Cambridge, occupation of sheet metal worker.

In September of 1939 there were many airfields in Cambridge and sheet metal was in great demand for the production and repair of aircraft for the second world war. This could explain why George is living there helping with the war effort but why were they not living together as man and wife between their marriage in 1934 and 1940 and possibly up to 1945? To the date of publication this is a mystery.

In 1905 a man with the name George Baxter was shown on the electoral roll as renting rooms at 30 Warren Street, the same address as Dorothy's uncle Herman. I think this must be a coincidence as this man would have been born some twenty to thirty years before Dorothy's husband George Baxter. It wasn't Dorothy's husband's father either as his name was Alfred.

I do believe that Dorothy's husband is the same George Baxter that was a witness to the marriage of Dorothy's brother William Bernard Hepting to Lilian Cartwright. The signatures of George Baxter on William's marriage certificate and the signature on Dorothy and

George's marriage certificate are the same.

In 1939 Dorothy was still shown as living with her father and siblings at 10 Howard House in Marylebone, although now finally shown as Dorothy Baxter. Was there an oversight or was there some other reason?

There were no electoral rolls or census details taken during the war years and so there is no information available for Dorothy and George throughout those years.

After the war and between 1945 and 1965 George and Dorothy were living at 53 Corinne Road in London and may have continued to do so after that date. They had one daughter Linda, born in London in early 1944.

George died in London in July 1995 aged eighty-five.

Dorothy died in London aged eighty-seven, in February 1997.

Harry Hepting was born on 4th September 1911. Harry was living at home with his siblings at 10 Howard House, Cleveland Street in London at the time of his marriage to Maud Kathleen Prosser in 1941 in Hammersmith. Albert Mark, his father, had died the previous year. Maud was born on 23rd May 1921. They moved to a flat at 178 Ladbroke Grove in London soon after their marriage and lived there for most, if not all, of their married life. I have found no record of any children born to the marriage.

Harry died aged sixty-seven on 5th April 1979 in London.

Sometime after Harry died his wife Maud moved to Ingestre Court in the same building as Louisa Frances Hepting. Although both Maud and Louisa Frances lived at Ingestre Court in London they each had their own flat.

Maud was with Louisa Frances in her flat when Sidney, Bill and Jim visited Louisa.

Maud died aged seventy-seven on 30th August 1998.

Maud (Prosser) Hepting

Frank Sidney

Son of Anthony and Louisa HEPTING

Frank Sidney Hepting was born in 1885 at 37 Newman Street in London. Frank was a hairdresser and lived at home with his family.

Frank aged just eighteen died in June 1903 of a reported burst appendix and cardiac failure.

Herman Adolph

Son of Anthony and Louisa HEPTING

Herman Adolph Hepting was born on 10th July 1881 at 37 Newman Street in London and was baptised on 31st August 1881 in the parish of St. Andrew, St. Marylebone, London.

It seems as though there was some confusion on the spelling of Adolph. On the original baptism record Adolfe is shown but on other records it's spelled as Adolph, Adolf and Adolphus. Adolphus is the English version of the same name. What spelling was intended by Anthony and Louisa is not known. The names they chose for their children were both English and German. The name of Herman Adolph though was more obviously German than his siblings' names.

As was the tradition in Germany, when a member of the family died the next born would often be given their name, so perhaps a relative had died and Herman was named after that person.

Herman was still living at 37 Newman Street, aged nineteen. Herman didn't follow in his father's footsteps as a clock and watchmaker choosing instead to become a French Polisher. He may have realised, from seeing his father's and uncle's businesses decline, that watches and clocks were now being mass produced and the profession, as his father knew it, was becoming less viable.

Herman married Kate Florence Hardy at the Register Office in St. Marylebone in London on 3rd July 1901. They went on to have three children.

On the marriage certificate Herman was shown as

being twenty-three years of age when in fact he was only nineteen. I believe that he lied about his age because he was under age to marry without the consent of his parents. Marriage was only legally allowed from the age of twenty-one without parental consent. Although why they wouldn't give him their consent is open to debate, perhaps they believed that Kate was older than she was telling and therefore not trustworthy.

Kate certainly lied about her age as she was shown as being twenty-six years old at the time of their marriage, three years older than Herman's 'age' shown. In fact Kate would have actually been thirty-five at the time of their marriage and sixteen years older than Herman's real age of nineteen. Why did she lie about her age? Did Herman know what age she was? Did his parents suspect? On the 1901 census, taken on 31st March, a few months before Kate married Herman, Kate is shown as being thirty-three! On the 1911 census, taken on 2nd April, she is shown as age thirty-nine, ageing only six years in ten - nice trick!

However, Kate was born on 13th June 1866, as shown on her birth certificate, and was in fact thirty-four in 1901 when the census was taken and forty-four in 1911. It seems strange that she continued to lie after their marriage which suggests that Herman was unaware of her real age.

Kate would have given birth to her daughter Janet at forty-two years of age. It's not known whether Herman knew Kate was older or why she felt she needed to lie about her age. Unless she didn't know how old she was, which is unlikely, lie she did!

Kate Florence Hardy was born in June 1866 to Mary Jane (Robbins) Hardy who was born in 1837 in Shillingstone, Dorset and John Hardy who was born in

1834 in Shaftesbury in Dorset. They married in the parish church of Sarum St. Edmunds, Salisbury in 1863. After their marriage, they lived in St. James Street, Shaftesbury in Dorset. St. James Street lies at the bottom of Gold Hill - the hill shown in the old Hovis loaf television advert, for those of you who remember it (the hill is not in Yorkshire as the advert has you believe).

Shaftesbury, Dorset

St. James Street

Ye Olde Two Brewers Inn

Gold Hill

John Hardy was a plasterer and in 1867, the year following Kate's birth, the family moved to London. (this was, coincidentally, the same year in which Anthony Hepting moved to London from Germany). There would have been more work opportunities for the family and no doubt suitors for their daughter. Mary Jane and John later had two more daughters.

Kate's sisters were Sarah Amy, and Mary Jane. Both her sisters seem to have been known by other names on different census and birth records. Sarah Amy was, from the first census after her birth, shown as Amy, on other census records she was shown as Emma and Sarah A! There is no doubt though that they are one and the same person. Mary Jane was shown on the 1881 census record as Janet. Perhaps they just liked to change their names or it's possible that the enumerator (the person who recorded the information on the completed forms onto the census books) either couldn't read the writing on the form or didn't hear if he was verbally given the information.

John Hardy died in 1917, aged eighty-three.

Mary Jane Hardy died in 1924, aged eighty-eight.

In 1903 Herman and Kate were living at 120 Great Titchfield Street, London and later moved to 30 Warren Street, London. Between 1906 and 1911 Herman and Kate had moved to 12 Church Road, Tottenham. The road was directly opposite the old Tottenham Hotspur football ground. Tottenham in 1911 was a much nicer place to live than central London. London was overcrowded and busy and Tottenham would then have been the countryside. The air would have been cleaner with plenty of green spaces, trees and fields all around and the roads would not have been as busy. Except perhaps on a Spurs match day! A much healthier place to raise children in those days.

By 1911 Herman and Kate had been married for ten years and had three children. Sidney William Charles, Frank Anthony John Herman and Janet Florence Louise.

Herman tried to join up in 1914 when world war one started but he was classified as medically unfit. Herman was advised by the Army that he was likely to become crippled in his old age. As he aged he did become immobile. His daughter Janet and son Frank worked for a company in Silver Street in Edmonton called Klingers, the factory made hosiery products, knitwear and other fabric goods. The owner/manager apparently heard about Herman's invalidity and bought him a tricycle. One wheel on the front and two on the back it was operated and steered with his hands. Herman loved it and used it to get about. According to his granddaughter Joan, her mother Janet told her that he may have enjoyed it a bit too enthusiastically as on one occasion he was brought home by the police as he was racing in it at Barnet and the tricycle tipped over! Joan believes there may also have been other incidents such as this.

In 1923 Herman and Kate's eldest son Sidney William Charles married Emily Adelaide Bedford.

According to his grandson Jim Hepting, Herman always wore a collarless pinstripe shirt with braces and a big, buckled leather belt too, together with black boots he looked just like Alf Garnett, the bigoted character from the TV series of 1965-1975 'Til Death Us Do Part'. He was nearly balding and on the plump side. Herman enjoyed showing the grandchildren little tricks with cards and coins and loved mending their toys for them.

In 1936 Herman and Kate's only daughter Janet Florence Louise married Frederick W C Sewell.

Herman died the following year in April 1937, aged

just fifty-five years.

In December 1937 Frank Anthony John Herman married Emily Ann Carter.

Kate, who was now seventy, continued to live at 12 Church Road. However, also shown at 12 Church Road, on the 1939 Register, were Kate's two sisters, Mary Jane and Sarah Amy. There was no census taken in 1941 or electoral rolls taken during the war years of 1940 to 1945 so it's impossible to say if Kate's sisters remained there throughout the war or if they only stayed there for a short time. Mary Jane was widowed and her married surname was Skinner. Sarah Amy was unmarried.

Sometime between September 1939 and an electoral roll taken in 1946 Kate's sisters had left and Kate was again living on her own at 12 Church Road.

Her daughter Janet was spending a lot of time going to her mother's house to help her and so Janet's husband Frederick suggested that Kate move in with them. By 1949 Kate was living with her daughter Janet and husband Frederick Sewell at 11 Chalfont Green in Edmonton, North London.

In 1960 Kate went into St. Michael's hospital in Chase Side, Enfield. Kate had fallen down the stairs, broken her hip and then got pneumonia in hospital. Probably to everyone's surprise, at the age of ninety-four, Kate recovered and returned home to 11 Chalfont Green.

Kate, having lived a long life, died in January 1963 aged ninety-six.

Kate Hardy

Frank Anthony John Herman

Son of Herman and Kate HEPTING

Frank Anthony John Herman Hepting was born on 10th October 1903 whilst Herman and Kate were living at 120 Great Titchfield Street, London W1. He was baptised on 22nd December 1903. Frank was born a few months after Herman's brother Frank Sidney had died. In keeping with German tradition, Herman and Kate named their son not only after Herman's brother Frank but also after their father (Anthony), his wife's father (John) and himself (Herman)!

Frank married quite late in life, staying at home until his marriage to Emily Ann Carter, who was born in May 1902.

Frank and Emily married in December 1937 in the Parish Church in Tottenham. This was later the same year in which Frank's father Herman had died. In 1939 Frank and Emily were living at 18 Branksome Avenue, Edmonton. Frank was shown as a machinist at Klingers hosiery (socks, stockings, knitwear etc.) factory.

By 1946 Frank and Emily had moved to 10 Church Road, next door to his mother Kate. Frank was very enterprising and used his front garden to store football supporters' bicycles on a Saturday when Spurs were playing at home. He charged sixpence (2.5p in today's money) a bike for the duration of the game. He'd buy a book of raffle tickets and place one part of the ticket on the bicycle and give one part to the owner. His nephews, Sidney's sons, would go to help their uncle Frank with storing the bikes and he would pay them one shilling.

Frank and Emily had one child, Ronald Frank who was born in early 1942.

Frank's wife Emily died in Edmonton in 1958 aged fifty-six when Ronald was just sixteen years old.

Emily (Carter) Hepting

In October 1963 Frank married Rose Adelaide (Sykes) Sims. Rose was born in 1906 in Mile End Old Town, London. Rose had previously married John Sims in 1927 in Poplar but John had passed away in 1957.

Frank married Rose at the Register Office in Poplar and they lived at 25 Autumn Street, Poplar. I'm not sure how they met as Tottenham and Poplar are not next door to each other!

Rose Adelaide passed away in late 1972, aged sixty-six.

Frank passed away seven years later, aged seventy-five, in 1979.

Ronald Frank

Son of Frank and Emily (Carter) HEPTING

Ronald Frank remained at 10 Church Road until he married Anne Marriott in 1964 in Edmonton. Ronald as a young lad had very blond hair and blue eyes and his cousins commented on how he looked stereotypically German. His father Frank used to take Ronald to his uncle Sidney and aunt Emily's house to watch his father, uncle and cousins playing on the dog board and would get very excited if his dad's dog was winning.

As an adult, Ronald was an engineer. He and his wife Anne had two sons.

Ronald Frank died on 15th October 2013, aged seventy-one, at the University Hospital, Stoke on Trent, Staffordshire.

Janet Florence Louise

Daughter of Herman and Kate HEPTING

Janet Florence Louise Hepting was born to Herman and Kate in January 1909 in Tottenham.

Janet married Frederick W C Sewell in October 1936. Frederick was born at 7 Graham Road, Edmonton in April 1913. In 1939 they were living at 11 Branksome Avenue, Edmonton a few doors away from her brother Frank and his wife Emily. Janet and Frederick later moved to 11 Chalfont Green in Edmonton. They had three children, two daughters, Joan and Janet (known as Jane) and one son, Frederick.

Janet's husband Frederick died in late 1966, aged fifty-three.

Janet and Frederick's daughter Joan was born in 1938. Joan married Stanley Rayner in 1955 and they settled in Australia when her husband was offered a job there. Stanley was born in 1924 and died in 2009.

Their son, Frederick J C Sewell was born in 1948 and married Jean Smith in 1969. Jean was born in 1948.

Janet and Frederick's daughter Janet Sewell was born in 1950. Jane told me that her mother Janet was very impish and fun loving and went to Australia to stay with her daughter Joan on several occasions.

By the time her mother Janet was eighty she knew all of the bus routes in Greater London, all of the public toilets and most of the tea shops. She was out every day and it was nothing for her to go to Cranfield Park in Ilford, Golders Green, Brent Cross, Brookfield Farm in Cheshunt, Oxford Street, Richmond, or Southend, all by bus, just to get a cup of tea and a jacket potato.

Janet had a long life, not passing until early 2002, at Barnet in Hertfordshire, aged ninety-three. Clearly Janet inherited her mother Kate's genes.

Janet and Frederick with their daughter Joan and Janet in later years

Memorial plaque to Janet and her husband

Janet and daughter Joan

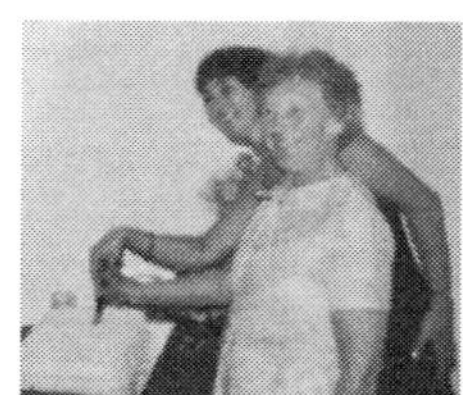

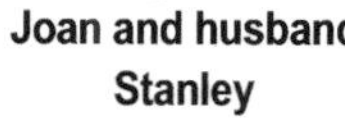

Joan and husband Stanley

Cousins – Jane, Barbara and Joan

Janet

Janet and Frederick's children – Joan, Frederick and Jane

Sidney William Charles

Son of Herman and Kate HEPTING

Sidney William Charles Hepting was born to Herman and Kate on 1st January 1902. In 1911 the family lived at 12 Church Road, Tottenham, North London. Sidney is aged nine, his brother Frank is aged seven and his sister Janet is aged two. Sidney was small in stature with dark brown hair in his youth, he had a fair complexion and a thin moustache. When Sidney was a young lad he went busking and step (tap) dancing at Monkey's Parade in Tottenham and would draw quite a crowd. This is where he met his future wife Emily.

In September 1923 Sidney was twenty-one and a French Polisher, following in his father's footsteps. In that year he married Emily Adelaide Bedford, then aged eighteen, at the Register Office in Edmonton. Emily was working as a domestic servant at that time.

When Sidney married Emily she was living at home in Tewkesbury Road, Tottenham. Following their marriage, Emily and Sidney shared the house with her mother and father.

The Bedford Family Tree

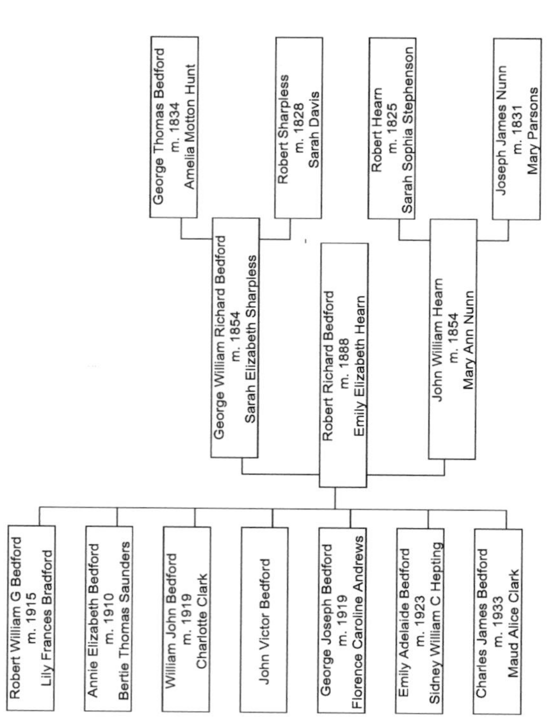

George Thomas Bedford
m. 1834
Amelia Motton Hunt
Robert Sharpless
m. 1828
Sarah Davis
Robert Hearn
m. 1825
Sarah Sophia Stephenson
Joseph James Nunn
m. 1831
Mary Parsons
George William Richard Bedford
m. 1854
Sarah Elizabeth Sharpless
Robert Richard Bedford
m. 1888
Emily Elizabeth Hearn
John William Hearn
m. 1854
Mary Ann Nunn
Robert William G Bedford
m. 1915
Lily Frances Bradford
Annie Elizabeth Bedford
m. 1910
Bertie Thomas Saunders
William John Bedford
m. 1919
Charlotte Clark
John Victor Bedford
George Joseph Bedford
m. 1919
Florence Caroline Andrews
Emily Adelaide Bedford
m. 1923
Sidney William C Hepting
Charles James Bedford
m. 1933
Maud Alice Clark

Emily Adelaide Bedford

Daughter of Robert and Emily (Hearn) Bedford

Emily Adelaide (Bedford) Hepting was born on 27th December 1904 to Robert Richard Bedford and Emily Elizabeth (Hearn) Bedford. Emily was a very strong, spirited lady. She was of average height with fine dark brown, wavy hair that she always wore in a bob just below the ears, her eyes were large and dark. Emily Adelaide had five brothers and one sister. Emily was close to her family, particularly to her only sister Annie. Annie's husband Bertie passed away in 1932 aged just forty-one leaving Annie to care for their six children. Annie also lost a daughter, Rosetta, in 1934 aged just nineteen. Rosetta had been working for the British Embassy in Paris until she became ill and was returned to England to the North Middlesex hospital in Edmonton, North London where she later died.

Emily married Sidney William Charles Hepting in 1923.

Emily was born in Tottenham and, apart from a few holidays in the UK and abroad, remained there her entire life.

If asked, Emily would happily tell of events in their

younger lives and when I was a young girl she told me that her mother's family were Irish. She also said that her mother used to tell her Irish folk tales and stories. I have researched extensively to find a link but have not found one to date. Emily's sister Annie also told her family the same story but nothing has yet come to light on who it was or when they came from Ireland. All the families to date are recorded as coming from London or other places in England but not Ireland. The name of Hearn can be found in Ireland and it may be that there is a connection going back. Neither Emily nor Annie would have told this story if they had not believed it to be true.

The twin sisters, Emily Adelaide's mother, Emily Elizabeth Hearn and her twin sister, Sarah Ann Hearn were born in 1864. The date of the birth is recorded on the baptism record four years later. There is also mention in the family of Emily Elizabeth and Sarah Ann being of triplets but only two survived. However as I cannot find any record of their births, twins or triplets, in England this can't be confirmed. There doesn't appear to be a birth registration for them in 1864. I have researched the Irish records but many of these were lost in a fire in Dublin.

It's possible the Hearn family was in Ireland for the birth of the twins but I can find no evidence of it and as far as the records show, they all lived in London. Certainly they were in London in 1861 and 1871 as shown on the census records for those years. They were also in London in 1862 when the first two of the Hearn's children died and Mary was born. In 1867 they were in London when Ellen was born. There is a gap between late 1862 and 1867 so were the family in Ireland then, if so, why were they there? The Hearn daughters baptisms took place in London in 1868, when all four of the Hearn girls were baptised together, Mary born 1862, Sarah Ann and Emily Elizabeth born 27th September 1864 and Ellen born in 1867.

It was common then to baptise children together to save on costs. Both of Emily Elizabeth's parents, John Hearn and Mary Ann (Nunn) Hearn, were according to census records also born in London as were their parents. It's possible the girls, Emily Elizabeth and Sarah Ann were born in Ireland and they didn't state this on the census records due to the stigma of being Irish at that time. Why they would have been in Ireland though when all the family appear to have been born and lived in London is a mystery.

Emily Adelaide (Bedford) Hepting

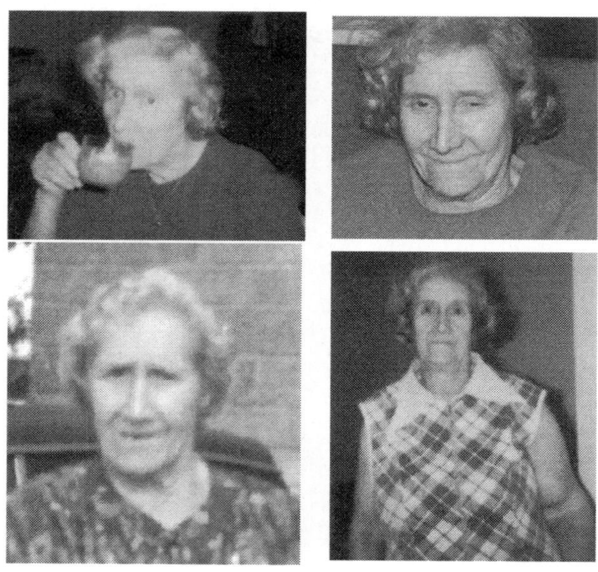

Emily Adelaide Bedford's parents

Robert Richard Bedford was born in October 1861 and was baptised in 1869. At the time the family were living at 12 Bear Lane in London. Robert was baptised in Christ Church, Southwark. This is just a short distance from Blackfriars Bridge in London. Robert and Emily Elizabeth were married in the Parish Church of Clerkenwell on 15th April 1888. Robert was a coppersmith. After their marriage they lived at various addresses and eventually moved to Tottenham.

Emily Elizabeth Hearn was born in September 1864 to John Hearn and Mary Ann (Nunn) Hearn. John Hearn and Mary Ann married on 25th December 1854 at St. Andrews Church, Bethnal Green, London. John was living at 20 Wilmot Street and Mary Ann was living at 12 Wilmot Street. John Hearn was a glass cutter.

Emily Elizabeth had four sisters and four brothers, Joseph William, Adelaide Amelia, Mary Jane, Sarah Ann, Ellen, John, William and Joseph.

Both Joseph William born in 1858 and Adelaide Amelia born in 1856 had died sometime in the three months to June 1862.

In 1868 Emily Elizabeth was baptised with her twin

sister Sarah Ann and her sisters Mary Jane and Ellen.

Emily Elizabeth Hearn's twin sister Sarah Ann married Robert Richard Bedford's brother, William Bedford. Emily Elizabeth and Sarah Ann later gave three of their children the same names too. That must have caused some confusion when referring to them in the family!

Robert and Emily Elizabeth (Hearn) Bedford

In 1901 Robert and Emily were living at 112 Tiverton Road but when Emily Adelaide was born in 1904 they had moved to St. Anne's Road and in 1911 were at 63 Tewkesbury Road, later moving to 52 Tewkesbury Road, Tottenham.

Robert and Emily Elizabeth (Hearn) Bedford had nine children, two of whom died in early childhood, the surviving children were Robert William, Annie Elizabeth, William John, John Victor, George Joseph, Charles James and Emily Adelaide. Robert was very strict and unfeeling, according to the grandchildren.

Emily Elizabeth died in April 1934 aged sixty-nine. She was laid to rest in Tottenham Cemetery grave number 1421 Western.

Robert Richard Bedford was admitted to Enfield House, Chase Side, Enfield, a geriatric hospital (later St. Michael's) and from there wrote to his daughter Emily Adelaide. The letter is undated but may have been written in 1947 or 1948. The letter does tell us a little about Robert's feelings at that time.

The following is a transcription of that letter. Some of it is unreadable due to the age of the letter and unfortunately the last part is also missing.

This is the transcription of the four pages that exist.

My Dear daughter
Just a line in answer to your very kind and welcome letter I was glad to hear that you and your family was quite well and that I was going to have some more great grandchildren that will make about 24 of them. I feel quite proud of myself to think I have lived so long but what a mob. I would like to come and see you but I am so ill and they won't let me come out I don't know if you know it but I have been very ill all this year. They thought it was all over ………?………. and they sent for Bob, he came that night and did not come anymore. She used to come on Sunday and always has a tale to tell about Bob so I wrote Bob a letter telling him off for not coming to see me and when ....?……. had been giving me so when she came on Sunday with a few things I sent them back. She has not been since. Bob, George and Charlie never come to see me. Your sister Annie and young Joan comes to see me ...?..... every Sunday, that is what was the matter with Lill she did not like to see my own come to see me. I would like to see you and then I could tell you about it as I can't tell you in this letter I can't spell what I did know I have forgot and that is why I want to see you as you can't come on Saturday and Sunday …………?…...... till 4 and if you do come try to bring 1 or 2 of your children with you I should like to see Bill and Barber I wish I could get out I would and see you but they won't let me out I am to ill Em you know this place is not what it was they have turned it into a hospital they are sending all the men and women away so many at a time to homes in the country but if they want me to go I shall take my discharge and come out and take my chance so I want you to come and see me as soon as you can and then I can tell you all about it……….

Robert Richard Bedford died in 1948 aged eighty-seven.

Emily Adelaide's grandparents and great grandparents

Robert Richard Bedford was born to George William Richard Bedford, a bricklayer and Sarah Elizabeth (Sharpless) Bedford. George and Sarah married on 25th December 1854 at St. Bride's Church, London. It wasn't uncommon for people to marry on Christmas Day as this was often the one day in the year that everyone was off work and so could attend family events. George William's father was George Thomas Bedford, born in 1816 and a dock labourer and his mother was Amelia Motton (Hunt) Bedford born in 1818 in Devonport, Devon. They married in 1834.

Emily Elizabeth Hearn was born to John William Hearn and Mary Ann (Nunn) Hearn. John was born in London on 9th June 1831 and baptised on 2nd April 1832. John earned his living as a glass cutter.

John's father, Robert Hearn was born in London in 1805 and was also a glass cutter. Robert Hearn died in 1872. John's mother was Sarah Sophia (Stephenson) Hearn who was born in 1806 and died in 1855, aged 49. Robert and Sarah married in St. Leonard's Church in Shoreditch, London on 20th November 1825.

John William Hearn passed away in 1907.

Mary Ann (Nunn) Hearn was born in London on 5th August 1834 to parents Joseph Nunn and Mary (Parsons) Nunn who had married in St. Leonard's Church, Shoreditch, London in November 1831.

Mary Ann (Nunn) Hearn passed away in 1897.

Sidney and Emily (Bedford) HEPTING

On the electoral roll of 1924 Sidney's father, Herman, was shown as Jack. This, my father Bill and uncle Jim both said, was because Emily's father was a staunch patriot and royalist and had sons in the British Army and he didn't like the idea of his daughter courting Sidney Hepting because Sidney's surname and his father's names, Herman Adolph Hepting, were of obvious German origin and so Herman called himself Jack. This, in spite of the fact that Sidney's uncle, Albert Mark, spent sixteen years in the British Army, long before and during the first world war. Similarly his cousin Harry had fought and died in 1916 in France fighting for the British Army. However because of Sidney's father's names and the anti-German feeling that remained after the first world war perhaps Emily's father thought life would be difficult for her if it were known of her father in law's name and origins.

Germans, during the first world war, and any person with a German name, would automatically have been viewed with suspicion. Most were interned during the world wars and although several years had passed since the end of the first world war, when Emily and Sidney married, there was still strong anti-German feeling.

In 1934 at 52 Tewkesbury Road, Tottenham it must have been getting very crowded as not only were Sidney and Emily living there with the first five of their children but in 1933 Emily's brother Charles married Maud Alice Clark and they were also living there!

In 1934 Emily and Sidney's sixth child James (Jim) was born. This was just a few months before Emily's mother, Emily Elizabeth, died. During 1935 or 1936 Charles and Maud moved out of the house, giving everyone a bit more room!

Emily and Sidney later had their own home but always lived in Tottenham. From Tewkesbury Road, they moved to 31 Station Road. Bill, my father, told me that the house was very crowded and the brothers had to share their beds with each other in one room and the girls had another bedroom. There were rat problems too being next to the railway station and the River Lea. They would often have rats in the bedroom at night which the brothers would try to catch. Later, when most of the older ones had married, those who were left at home moved to a maisonette above a small parade of shops at 143 High Cross Road, Tottenham. The maisonettes still stand there but High Cross Road is no longer a through road to the High Road in Tottenham as it once was.

Between 1923 and 1950 Emily and Sidney had nine sons and five daughters. Sidney Robert, Emily Margaret (known in the family as Sissy), Frank Terence, Stanley Victor (always called Bill by the family but Pepper by his friends), Ann Barbara (always known as Barbara), Leslie Charles, Sylvia Gwendolyn, James William (Jim), Kenneth Roy (Ginger), Beryl Rosemary, Ronald Edward, Bernard Alexander (Monty), Raymond Douglas

(Cod) and Marlene. Emily was forty-five when she had Marlene and said that she was born with severe Down's Syndrome. Marlene sadly died a month after her birth.

Emily had great strength of character and great mental fortitude, no doubt resulting from a tough upbringing and the difficult life that she had lived. Looking after and taking care of all their children must have been a never ending task. Not to mention doing much of this in an overcrowded environment and all by hand, there were no automatic gadgets or washing machines then!

Living through the second world war in constant fear of having bombs and fire bombs falling must have felt like a nightmare. There was also the need to evacuate the youngest children to live with strangers to keep them safe from the bombing raids. This must have caused Emily great distress and concern. Food was always in short supply. During the war with the shortages and so many mouths to feed it would have been a near impossible task. With rationing in place, coupons were issued to buy the essentials. There were queues for everything and sometimes when you reached the front of the queue there would be nothing left in the shops or only food that no-one else wanted because it would be substandard. The children would often have bread and dripping for their meals. Dripping was the meat juices and fat left over from roasting a joint of meat that solidified after an hour or so. You could buy this very cheaply at the butchers and was a staple of the poor.

There was devastation everywhere caused by the bombs and fires. Windows blown out, houses in ruin and the rubble lying in the streets, once the homes of family, friends and neighbours. Fires would be raging from the incendiaries and from blown gas mains, the smell of gas escaping everywhere must have been horrific. When the air raid sirens sounded people would have to take cover from the falling bombs in the London Underground stations or in the inadequate garden shelters that had been supplied. The garden shelters were not designed to protect people from the direct hit of a bomb but rather to protect them against falling shrapnel and glass from bombed buildings.

Bombings often happened at night and in most cases the Underground was the safest place as sometimes the raids went on for hours. Many though wouldn't go to the Underground for fear of being buried alive. Those that did go would sing songs to try and raise the spirits of the young and themselves. Some would play their accordions or mouth organs, trying to keep the children from being scared. Worst of all was the loss of family, friends and neighbours to the raids or in the fighting overseas. Huge air balloons (barrage balloons) hung in the skies over the cities. Everywhere, including schools, remained open and were attended by those children who hadn't been evacuated.

Despite the risks, Emily told me that as time went on in the early part of the war when the bombs didn't immediately come she, like many other mothers, brought some of the older children back home. The children had been evacuated to Cornwall, Norfolk, Wales and other rural places to keep them safe. In 1940 and 1941 though, the bombs eventually came (this was known as the Blitz). Night after night of bombing raids were endured and this was the bombing that had been forecast, albeit later than expected.

In 1944 came the horror of the V1 and V2 rockets (the doodlebugs) launched from the Hague with just enough fuel to reach their intended target. You were safe if you could hear the engine of the rocket but once the engine cut out it was time to find cover because it meant that the rocket had run out of fuel and was coming down. The only thing you could do was to take cover and hope that it didn't land near you.

Jim related a story of what happened to him and his brother Leslie when a doodlebug fell close to them as they were playing on a bombsite. His story is in the family memories section at the back of this book.

Sidney was an air raid warden during the second world war. His duties were to patrol the streets during the blackout and ensure that no lights were showing. If a light was seen he would shout 'put that light out' or 'cover that window.' He would also have reported bomb damage to the authorities and assessed the local need for the emergency services. Air raid wardens were responsible for handing out gas masks if someone didn't have their own with them, directing people to air raid shelters in a raid and arranging for the ordering of pre-fabricated air raid shelters such as Anderson shelters. The wardens also organised and staffed public air raid shelters. When bombs had fallen they would help people out of the destroyed houses and shelters and assist the emergency services to search for casualties. They would have used their knowledge of the local area to help find and reunite family members who had been separated in the rush to find shelter from the bombs.

There were many men who, for one reason or another, were unable to go and fight and so continued their day jobs while helping the war effort by volunteering as air raid wardens and fire watchers. Fire watchers would put out incendiaries, small firebombs like large fireworks, as they fell either on the buildings or to the ground to prevent them causing fires.

Emily would give Sidney a flask of tea and some sandwiches or bread and dripping for the night on duty. On quiet nights the air raid wardens would sit playing cards to pass the time.

During raids, if a household like the Hepting family had too many children at home to fit into the garden air raid shelter during a raid, neighbours would lift some of the children over the fence and the children would sit with the neighbours in their shelter until the raid was over. Everyone helped one another as much as they could. Emily said that people also shared what little food they had with their neighbours if they were in need.

After coming through the war relatively unscathed and with the family all together again, the daily struggle continued. The children that had been away for most of the war had to get re-acquainted with their family again.

Emily made some of the children's clothes to save money but never complained despite the heavy burden of family work that she carried. Emily was obviously made of tough stuff.

In the 1950s Emily had breast cancer and had an operation to remove her left breast which left her with a double sized arm due to the reaction on the lymph nodes. The procedure wasn't as advanced then as it is today and she used to call it her fat arm. Emily never complained about it, instead joked that it was heavier than the other one and good for hitting Raymond with when he teased her too much, she'd say with a wink. The chances of surviving breast cancer then were much lower than today and there wasn't the support that there is now either but of course Emily just got on with it as always.

Although the family had very little, Emily was nonetheless proud. As mentioned in Ronald Edward Hepting's book of his life, he once told his friends that their cups were jam jars and when it got back to his mother, he took a walloping for that truth. It wasn't the 'done thing' to talk about what you did or didn't have or to talk about the family to outsiders, no matter who they were. Family business was just that and not for common knowledge or gossip. Emily had very strong principles and always stuck to them.

Emily and Sidney's front door was always open and all were welcome. No-one had to call before they visited, just turn up, walk in and you would be welcomed with a cup of strong tea and a piece of Emily's home-made bread pudding. All who remember Emily's bread pudding loved it and said it was the best there is, there was always a large tray of it in the kitchen. Emily's daughter Barbara told me that her husband Frank always said how much he liked her mum's bread pudding and cooking. The tea though was a different matter for me, you could stand your spoon up in it, it was very strong! That's how they liked to drink it.

Sidney was always telling jokes or doing little tricks to amuse all the grandchildren that would visit them. He would do a trick that he called 'raising the donkey's tail' with matches and a matchbox. He would also make a sixpence (an old small silver coin) appear from behind our ears. Sidney and Emily had a budgie and Sidney would call to it and it would fly down and sit on his shoulder, hop onto his finger and appear to dance when Sidney whistled a tune.

The home was full of laughter, teasing, playing pranks on one another and great debates which sometimes became a little heated and an argument would brew up but it never lasted for long.

The brothers and their dad had jamming sessions in the lounge, dad Sidney would be on drums, Ginger, Ron and Ray on guitars, Bill on his mouth organ, Jim on the comb (a cigarette paper folded over a comb, it was then put to the mouth and blown onto), quite effective in the right hands, and son Sidney played the washboard.

Some of the brothers and dad Sidney formed a skiffle group, playing at local venues and entering music competitions. During the 1960's the brothers would get together and play snooker at home on a table that was almost as big as the lounge with just enough room to walk around. Often the brothers would be playing snooker and an argument would break out but it was quickly resolved.

They also played the greyhound race game that eldest son Sidney had made. Cards, draughts and dominoes were often played too, having a penny bet on each game to make it more interesting. I don't remember if they had a TV but if they did it was never on, they all made their own entertainment. If they weren't playing a game they would be having a debate.

Sidney passed away in 1968, aged sixty-six.

After Sidney's death Emily stoically carried on and once a week went to a general warehouse to buy goods to sell from home to earn some money. Emily bought a varied selection of items to sell: socks, stockings, underwear, perfumes, soaps, bath salts, creams and lotions etc. It was very useful, particularly at Christmas, to be able to buy presents that we wanted from Emily who lived just across the road to our house at Tottenham Hale. There was no internet, online or telephone ordering in those days and so Emily's home 'store' was really useful. Raymond, one of the younger sons, would often take her in his car to the warehouse but if he wasn't able to, she would happily go on the bus with her trolley, despite her advancing years.

Emily also told me the story that husband Sidney had told her about his great-grandfather being German and how as a six year old boy he had been adopted and taken the name of Hepting in Germany. Neither she nor Sidney knew anything more about it. This we now know was Anton that they were talking about.

Emily also related stories of how the family survived throughout the war and of their children growing up.

Despite the hardships Emily endured I never once heard her complain and she was never heard to say a bad word about anyone. If she disapproved of something or someone she would wrinkle her nose and sniff if anyone mentioned them. Without saying anything you knew she was not impressed.

Emily had a very busy life and in later years would sometimes join her sons and daughters and their partners in the local pub, the City Arms, opposite her maisonette in High Cross Road, Tottenham. Emily enjoyed a Mackeson or the occasional Guinness, she said that it was good for the health and she had been given it in hospital after delivering her children. Emily, if encouraged, would sing, at her seat with her Mackeson, and everyone joined in, she had a good, strong, melodious voice.

Emily at age sixty-seven travelled to Athens, Greece to be at her son Ken and daughter in law Roula's wedding in 1972. Not a big deal to travel to Greece today at sixty-seven but fifty years ago it was considered quite adventurous. She returned there on several occasions to see her son Ken and Roula. Emily was not afraid of anything or anyone, as her son Ronald related in his book.

As Emily aged, climbing the flights of stairs leading

to her maisonette was becoming difficult and Emily moved, with her son Monty who was now living with her after his divorce, to a new house in Hanover Road, Tottenham. There were still stairs in the house but at least it was only one flight instead of three!

Emily died in February 1984, aged seventy-nine.

There was a big family funeral with standing room only in the chapel at Enfield Crematorium. The chapel was full of the family and all those who knew Emily. Some long-standing members of the local police force also attended, dressed appropriately in dark suits, although they stayed at a distance. I like to think they attended as a mark of respect for the matriarch of an old, well known, large Tottenham family.

Emily was a warm, independent, bright, clever and wise woman who had a ready wit and always had time for everyone. She lived all her life in Tottenham. According to her children, Emily was strict with them, having many rules and never wavering but all agree that she was always fair.

Each of the children of Emily and Sidney had their talents, most came from necessity, others from choice.

At the time work opportunities for women were not as varied as today and were usually in cleaning, factory, shop or office jobs. Marriage and children usually followed a short spell of working. Men had to find work to support themselves and their families. Everyone was expected to work and contribute and it was no different for Emily and Sidney's children. Family roles in the mid to late twentieth century were still traditional, the wife staying at home to look after the children and the men going out to work and often to the pub after work. Emily's life was much the same but with many more children to raise than most!

Children of Sidney and Emily (Bedford) Hepting

Sidney Robert was born in August 1923 and grew up in Tottenham. Before Sidney married he had lived in Tewkesbury Road and 31 Station Road with his parents and brothers and sisters. Today Station Road is hardly recognisable since the redevelopment of the area leading to Tottenham Hale Tube/Rail/Bus station.

In 1939 at the start of the war Sidney was working as a French Polisher. Sidney joined the British Army when he was seventeen in 1940 and later joined the paratroopers regiment. At one stage he was in the Royal Artillery stationed at Woolwich Arsenal barracks until he was shipped out to the middle east. When the war was over and Sidney was discharged from the service he returned home to Tottenham and continued working as a French Polisher. Some years later when that work dried up he turned his hand to working as a painter and decorator.

In 1958 Sidney married Sarah Jane Murphy. Sarah was born in 1933 and was known as Jane to the family. In a strange repeat of family history Jane already had a son named Anthony. When Sidney and Jane married, Anthony was nearly three years old and was subsequently adopted by Sidney. The situation is similar to that of Lorenz Hepting and Gertrud Kirner one hundred and thirty-two years earlier in 1826, the child's name of Anton also being just a variation of Anthony. I don't believe that Sidney was aware of the full details of Lorenz, Gertrud and Anton's story at the time as most of the details have only come to light through research over the years since his passing.

Sidney and Jane added to their family and had five daughters. The family lived in Tottenham for many years but later moved to Hemel Hempstead, Hertfordshire where there was more space and cleaner air.

Sidney Robert like most, if not all, of the Hepting brothers liked a bet on the races. Sidney designed and made the 'dogs' game that was often played. Many of the family will remember this game. Sidney and the family used to have sessions with the game at their mum and dad's home in Tottenham. The game consisted of an oblong board on to which Sidney Robert had drawn and painted an oval dog track, Sidney also made the dogs, each on a stand, painted with different colours and numbers on them. Each of the starting squares had a number of 1-6 to represent the dog traps and lanes. It was a complete representation of the greyhound track.

Each player, at the outset of the game, would pick their dog and give a forecast for the race. A dice was used to move the dog around the track and the person to get to the winning post first was the winner. Each player bet with pennies and there were two kitties to be won. Each game had a kitty to be won for the first to reach the winning post. The second kitty would be won by the person who had the correct forecasts written down. Sidney Robert really should have sold his game, it would have been a hit, particularly at that time when dog racing was very much in fashion. Many of the family remember the fun, excitement, laughter and occasional argument that brewed up when it was being played.

The game was passed down to Sidney and Jane's daughters and it is still played by them occasionally.

Sidney Robert passed away in 2001, aged seventy-eight.

Jane passed away in 2010, aged seventy-seven.

Sidney in the army

Sidney and his wife Jane

Sidney impersonating Sammy Davis Jnr.

Emily Margaret (Sissy), was born in 1925 and married Walter (Wally) Woodroffe in early 1942. Wally was born in 1922 and was a general labourer in 1939. Emily was working as a spring mattress assembler at that time. Sissy and Wally had eight children, six daughters and twin sons.

When Sissy realised she was expecting a child at 45 she was initially concerned but after consulting with her doctor she was told that all was well. Sissy wrote an article about her unexpected pregnancy which was published in a popular women's magazine of the time.

After the initial worries and thoughts of possible issues that could arise due to the late age pregnancy and birth, all the family were excited and looking forward to a baby in the house. Their daughter was born healthy and well.

Emily passed away in 2011, aged eighty-five.

Walter was aged ninety when he passed away the following year in 2012.

Emily and Walter had been married for sixty-nine years.

Sissy

Wally and Sissy

Wally

Stanley Victor (Bill) was born in 1927, in Tottenham. Bill was evacuated to Cornwall, together with Jim, Frank and Leslie for a few years during the second world war. He enjoyed his time there with the fresh air and good home grown food. Bill was able to go and see Jim as although they were all billeted in different houses they were able to get together sometimes. Bill said that the people were good to him in his temporary home. The older boys were brought back to London in early 1944 when the threat of invasion was less likely. Many years later Bill, his wife Barbara and their youngest daughter often holidayed in Perranporth, close to where Bill had been evacuated.

Bill, as a young lad, had to find work when he returned from Cornwall and so he took a job in a laundry at the end of Tewkesbury Road. A year before the end of the war, in October 1944, Bill, aged sixteen, signed up to the Merchant Navy. I asked him why he'd signed up and he said that it was to have some 'adventures'.

When Bill entered the service he was five foot nine inches tall with brown hair and eyes and a fresh complexion. He was taken on as steward's boy and left as catering boy in April 1945. Bill had spells in the Merchant Navy and the Army. After April 1945 he was placed on attachment to the military police in Palestine.

Bill didn't enjoy being away from home saying it was quite different to England. Whilst in Palestine he spent a short while in 'jankers', the term for military jail, as he hadn't returned for duty on time and so was punished! Bill wasn't really cut out for the military life but stayed his term and with war long over by 1948 he left the service and settled down to finding a job back home in Tottenham. When I asked him about his time there he said that it was too hot, dry and dusty and he never wanted to go abroad again and couldn't see the attraction when comparing it to England. He never left England again after returning home. Bill took jobs painting and decorating but also took on labouring work to earn a wage.

After Bill had passed away and before his brother Jim passed away I asked Jim how Bill came about his nickname of Pepper. Jim said that although Bill never went looking for trouble, it sometimes found him. One evening whilst they were at the local snooker rooms there was an argument when a local amateur boxer, who was known as the 'Bear', wanted to use the snooker table before they'd finished their game. Bill wouldn't be intimidated. It turned into an argument and the boxer threw a punch, Bill had a bloody nose and so retaliated, knocking his adversary down. A friend of Jim's, there at the time, said that Bill was 'hot stuff' meaning he could throw a good punch. This is apparently where Bill's nickname 'Pepper' came from. Bill's motto in life was never start a fight, always walk away, but if that doesn't work, make sure you're the one to finish it and you'll never be bothered again. Both his sons also inherited the nickname although neither knew how it had come about. Some of my cousins, I've since learned, used to call our nan, Emily Hepting, Nanny Pepper.

Whether this was from hearing the story about Bill and they started calling his mum Nanny Pepper or whether there was another reason for her nickname I couldn't say.

A while after coming out of the Army, Bill met his wife to be, Barbara Lilian Ward, in a coffee/music bar in West Green Road, Tottenham. Barbara was born in 1933 and was training to be a hairdresser. Barbara was, by the time she met Bill, nearing the end of her apprenticeship. There was no pay, only tips that customers gave her. This was quite common for apprenticeships in those days, particularly in hairdressing. Barbara had one sister who passed away aged forty-nine years.

Barbara's mother and father weren't keen on Bill at the time, they thought that the boys of the big Tottenham family were 'spivs' and not good enough for their daughter! However, after much turmoil, they were married in 1951 when Barbara was eighteen. Barbara and Bill had five children, three girls and two boys.

While living at Tottenham Hale and before the family moved to Waltham Abbey, Bill liked to go to the City Arms pub just along the road from his home. He would meet up with some of his brothers and they would play darts or cards for the evening. The wives would sometimes join them.

Bill worked as a painter and decorator for most of his life but did a number of jobs to bring in the money. When outside work dried up during the winter, he worked on renovations or labouring. Bill also worked with his brother Ron for a short time in Waltham Abbey on a new housing estate that had been built.

In the early seventies the family moved from Tottenham and lived in one of the houses in Waltham

Abbey that Bill had worked on.

In his later years Bill turned his hand to cleaning on the London Underground. This was night work and anyone who has ever worked nights will tell you, it upsets the body clock and eating habits. Bill didn't like the job, working all night, but he stuck at it to bring in a wage until he retired.

Bill liked a 'flutter' on the horses and dogs when he had a spare bit of money, which wasn't often. He did have a couple of big wins, several hundred pounds twice on the horses and once on the dogs. The wins always came when money was particularly tight and things were looking desperate, guardian angels perhaps? The win on the dogs was the same when he went with his brother Jim to Haringey Dog Stadium one Christmas.

The stadium opened the year Bill was born in 1927, drawing a crowd of 35,000 on its first night. Dog racing was big business then and was very popular for many years. However, once online betting started trackside numbers began to drop and the stadium was sold and demolished in 1987. It's now a housing estate. Many dog stadiums went the same way. Bill gave his winnings to his wife Barbara, keeping some back to buy her a nice present and giving some money to his children.

In his retirement, he bought a metal detector and went to Epping Forest to see what he could find buried beneath the forest floor. Needless to say he found lots of different things from old bottles to shoe buckles but nothing of any value, to his disappointment.

Bill and his brother Jim believed that dog racing was fixed or that there was a system to winning more regularly. Bill spent many an hour during his retirement reading the Sporting Life paper and inputting race results and dog form into his computer. He would then analyse it all trying to find a system that would give him some big wins. He rarely made a bet during this time but would study 'form' and regularly discussed his findings with his brother Jim, either on the phone or by letter, and with anyone else who would listen.

Jim and Bill were interested in learning about their family history and went to London together many times, sometimes with brother Sidney, in search of information. After they found further details they would then obtain the birth, marriage or death certificates for confirmation that they had the right person and learn details of the earlier generation. In particular, they did what they could at the time to locate information about Anton (Anthony) their great grandfather, who settled in London in 1867. All information had to be researched in person in London at Somerset House. Most records have now been relocated to Kew but today almost everything is also available online.

Bill also loved discussions and debates and would talk about any subject with anyone who was willing. We had some great debates about every possible subject and they could go on for hours. They were often about subjects for which there were no answers but we just enjoyed the discussion.

Bill also had a good voice and played the mouth organ very well too. His favourite group was the Inkspots. His favourite 'modern' record was 'Vincent' by Don McLean.

Bill passed away in February 1999, aged seventy-one.

Barbara and Bill were married for forty-seven years on his passing.

Barbara joined Bill, passing away suddenly at the age of eighty-four in June 2017.

Bill in the Navy

Bill in the army

Bill in Palestine

Bill's wife Barbara

Youthful Barbara and Bill

Enjoying a pint

Family function

Family wedding

Family wedding

Frank Terence was born in July 1930. According to Jim Hepting, Frank was the image of Herman Hepting and said, 'see Frank and you see Herman'.

Frank was also evacuated to Cornwall during the early part of the war and was billeted on a farm there. He went at the same time as Jim, Leslie and Bill but they were all billeted separately. After the war and back in Tottenham, Frank met his wife to be, Vilma Kilrow at the Royal (a dance hall) in Tottenham. Vilma was born in 1929. They married in 1948 and had one daughter.

Frank and Jim were close and their families used to meet on a Friday night in the City Arms pub in High Cross Road, Tottenham where the brothers played shove halfpenny, darts and cards while their wives and Frank's daughter chatted. They lived in Stoke Newington for many years before moving to Erith in Kent. Frank and Jim then kept in touch by phone and letter after he moved. Frank's work over the years included stockbroker, glassblower and toymaker. In their younger years Jim and Frank looked alike as can be seen from the picture of them later in this book.

Frank passed away in December 2002 aged seventy-two.

Vilma joined Frank, passing in October 2017, aged eighty-eight.

Frank and Vilma

Frank and daughter

Frank

Vilma and daughter

Leslie Charles Hepting was born in 1933. Leslie was also evacuated to Cornwall with Bill, Jim and Frank. Jim called him the lone wolf.

Leslie spent a few terms in prison. Leslie said that he only took from the 'establishment'. Because of the life he'd chosen to lead his mother would not allow him to live at home. Emily was very principled and honest and regardless of who you were, she stuck to those principles. Emily said that what he did was wrong and he was not welcome in the house. He sometimes visited his brothers and kept in touch with Jim in later years by text. He understood and respected his mother's decision not to have him at home.

Leslie married Jean Pavelin in 1967. Jean was born in 1945. This marriage ended and he later married for a second time to Doreen Wilsher in 1973. This marriage also ended. No children were recorded to either marriage.

Leslie lived in Nottingham for many years but kept in touch with his brothers and occasionally visited them.

Leslie passed away in Nottingham in November 2010 aged seventy-seven.

Leslie in his youth

James William (known as Jim) was born in January 1934 at the North Middlesex Hospital in Edmonton, London.

Jim said that one of his first memories, even though he was only a few months old, was of his grandmother Emily Elizabeth Bedford laying ill in her bed just before she passed away at home in 1934.

After the start of the second world war Jim, together with brothers Frank, Leslie and Bill, was evacuated to Goonhavern in Cornwall.

After the war, as a young lad, Jim would go along to his uncle Frank's house in Church Road, Tottenham on a Saturday to earn himself some money. He helped his uncle to store the bicycles of the Spurs supporters in his front garden and at the same time visited his grandmother Kate next door.

Jim told me that his grandmother Kate kept twelve cats at home. He said that every stray in the area would make their way to her house. Perhaps it's true what they say about cats being good for your health as Kate was ninety-six when she passed away!

Jim also visited his Aunt Lou (Great Aunt Louisa Christina) in Edmonton and said that she was always smiling, friendly and softly spoken and would give him a shilling and some sweets each time he visited.

Jim married Doreen Holmes in 1957. Doreen was

born in 1941 in Walthamstow. They had three sons. Their eldest son sent me a picture of a cuckoo clock that his wife had bought him for his birthday. It's an original cuckoo clock made by Fidel Hepting in the Black Forest (a picture of it is in the photo section of this book).

Jim and Doreen lived in Walthamstow for most of their married life. Jim was a painter and decorator but in his spare time and in retirement he liked to grow his own vegetables on his allotment. Over the years he won many prizes for his produce and said that whilst he loved being at home with Doreen he also enjoyed getting out in the air and spending time outside growing their food. Jim liked to keep busy and fit and rode his bicycle to the charity shop in Walthamstow where he worked as a volunteer.

Jim was a joker and often made up little humorous stories about our ancestors, either those back in the Black Forest or those in London in the middle 1800's and sent them to Bill in letters, before the advent of email. Jim often ended his letters about the family history by signing off as Herr Hepting in 'old' German script. He had taught himself the basics from books so that he could read and understand the family information and documents that he had obtained from Germany.

Jim, like many in the family, liked to write and often wrote to the papers to put his views on all manner of subjects. When the BBC asked the public for stories of the blitz Jim responded and wrote an article which was published on the BBC website. Jim sent the article to me for inclusion into the family book and this is shown in the Family Stories and Memories section.

Jim and his brother Sidney started researching the

family history many years ago and were joined by Bill, which then re-ignited my interest in our family story. Jim started the research from Anthony's and Herman's memorial cards and worked backwards from the information given on them. Jim said that he visited both grave sites in Tottenham cemetery but they are now just patches of grass with no headstones or other indications of the graves ever being there.

Bill and Sidney went with Jim on a number of occasions to London to further their research and to see their first cousin once removed, Albert Mark's daughter, Louisa Frances. She had lived in central London all her life and had never married. She gave Bill, Sidney and Jim information about Herman and her grandfather Anthony. Sidney, Jim and Bill spent many hours researching the family over the years, both at home and at Somerset House (then housing all the records) in London. Jim also paid a German genealogist to obtain copies of the birth and marriage documents for Anton (Kirner) Hepting to learn about the family history going back to the early 1800's in the Black Forest.

After Bill and Sidney had passed away Jim and I continued the research online, swapping bits of information by email as we found them. By this time the internet had grown and there were many family history websites online which made searching for the family connections that little bit easier. Even when Jim was ill he continued to spend time looking for information about the family and we'd share anything that we found.

Jim passed away in November 2014, in his eighty-first year.

Doreen and James had been married fifty-seven years on his passing.

Doreen and Jim in their youth

Doreen and Jim
relaxing in the garden

Jim the fisherman

It was this big!

Jim and Doreen with the awards for his allotment produce

Fishing in the snow – Luvvly Jubbly!

Ronald Edward was born in 1936 in Tottenham. Ron tells his own story in a true and frank book of his life called 'Farewell Mr John', published in 2019 and available from Amazon.

Ron had an interesting but at times turbulent life. After meeting at their workplace, Ron married Ruby Moles in early 1959. Ruby was born in 1940. They had three children, one girl and two boys and lived in Cheshunt, Hertfordshire for many years. Ron and Ruby later divorced and Ruby re-married in 1977.

Ruby passed away in November 2014, aged seventy-four.

Ruby

Ron always kept busy and in his spare time he entertained with his guitar, singing in some local pubs in Cheshunt, Hertfordshire, where he lived.

Ron was a worker and always managed to find work, doing several different jobs in the course of each day.

Ron, many years ago now, asked if I was able to help him to put his life story into book form and I gladly accepted the challenge. He explained that he wanted to write his life story as a legacy for his children so that future generations of his family would remember and know him through his book. Ron completed all the notes for his book and I had the privilege to edit and arrange publication for him.

Ron, as mentioned in his book, had been battling cancer and after further treatment and whilst in hospital, caught Covid19 in March 2020. Unaware that he had contracted the virus the hospital sent him home to live with his son. Within a day Ron started to have difficulty in breathing and was re-admitted to hospital for treatment where the virus was diagnosed. The family were all surprised and happy that Ron, against all the odds, survived Covid19 but he sadly remained ill due to the terminal cancer. After recovering from Covid19 in hospital Ron went to live in a nursing home where he was able to receive the daily care he needed.

After several months in the nursing home, on 9th July 2020, Ron passed away aged eighty-three.

Ron Hepting

Ann Barbara (always known as Barbara) was born in 1938 and married Frank Saville in 1959. Frank was born in 1935. Frank and Barbara had three children, two girls and one boy. Barbara was always kind and always smiling.

Barbara worked in an office before her marriage. After their marriage Barbara worked for Frank helping him with the office administration of his business. When they had their children Barbara continued to work for Frank but also did some homeworking jobs whilst she brought up their three children before they were of school age.

Barbara was always available and willing to look after her nieces and nephews. Whenever we were at her home she would let us all help her with the homeworking job that she did. One of the jobs that Barbara did was placing the small round piece of waxed card into the bottle tops for Lenthéric perfume bottles. There were thousands of the tops in a big cardboard box that had to be completed and then placed into another box once finished. We enjoyed doing this task and Barbara always gave us money for helping.

Frank was a heating engineer and ran his own business. He was a great joker with his nieces and nephews and was a kind man.

One of Barbara's grandchildren purchased a DNA

test for Barbara knowing that she was interested in the family history. The results showed that she was 96.7% British and 3.3% Greek and southern Italian. Barbara said that she was disappointed that it didn't show any Irish or German DNA as she knew her father's origins were German and Barbara also believed that her mother's origins were Irish.

Barbara used a mobile phone, computer, laptop and iPad to keep in touch with the wider family on Facebook and others by email. Barbara was very modern and forward thinking in her outlook and easily adapted to change.

The family lived in Beaconsfield Road in Tottenham all their married life until Frank's passing and Barbara continued to live there alone until her own passing.

Frank passed away in 2012, aged seventy-seven.

Barbara passed away in March 2020, aged eighty-two.

A note on DNA Testing

DNA tests are best taken by males of the family line to trace blood lineage as they show both maternal and paternal DNA whereas the female DNA test can only show the female lineage.

DNA tests for ancestry purposes only trace back eight generations and these tests that are analysed by most ancestry companies compare genetic material other than the male and female DNA. They look at the genetic similarities in other populations around the world.

In fact most people with white skin in England will have 25% German and 45% French genes within their DNA. This came about due to the settlement of German and French speaking peoples in Britain many generations ago.

Barbara's DNA, if a 'genetic' test was carried out, would be unlikely to show German as it was her father's line that was of German heritage and not her mother's. Female genetic DNA only shows the mother's DNA and not the father's lineage.

Ray, Monty and Barbara

Frank

Always smiling

Sylvia Gwendolyn was born in 1939. Sylvia was known in the family as Sylvie. Sylvie worked as a machinist after leaving school and in 1959 she married Thomas Pickley. They had two daughters. Sylvie and Tom lived in London during their married life. Sylvie and Tom subsequently divorced.

Sylvie later married Michael Kelly and they had one son. They later divorced.

Sylvie was fun loving and enjoyed a game of darts, as did most of the family.

Sylvie always dressed well and as a young girl I remember thinking that she looked like a movie actress as she always had perfectly applied make-up, perfectly arranged hair and looked very smart.

She can be seen in a picture on the following page collecting first prize in a darts competition.

When asked, Sylvie shared her memories of when she was young and these are in the Family Memories section in the back of this book.

Sylvia continues to live in London at the date of publication.

Sylvie winner of a darts competition

Beryl Rosemary was born in 1940 and worked as an office clerk and later in a school helping children with disabilities. In 1959 when Beryl was nineteen she married George Newson. George was born in 1936. Beryl and George had five children, three boys and two girls, there were two sets of twins and a single birth. Carole, one of the babies of the second set of twins, sadly died before her first birthday.

Beryl visited her mum in Tottenham regularly. On the many occasions that I saw Beryl at her mum's she was always smiling and enjoyed a good laugh. She was forthright and always spoke her mind, was always smartly but simply dressed and didn't worry about what people thought of her. She was, like her mother, a very strong person. Beryl and George later divorced.

George passed away in 2013.

In 1978 Beryl married Robert Campbell and they had a son. They later divorced.

Beryl passed away on 17th March 2019, aged seventy-eight.

Beryl and George on their wedding day

Kenneth Roy (Ginger) was born in 1942. On one occasion when Ken was young he almost got into a lot of trouble. He had been set upon by some boys near his home, apparently they had started a fight with him. When it was over he went home in a bit of a state. His brothers asked him what had happened. He told them and they said in future 'hammer' them back. Ken was quite young and angry at the time and took this literally, he went and got a hammer from the toolbox. Fortunately he was seen walking down the road with it in his hand and his brothers went and stopped him. When they asked him what he was doing, he said, just what you told me to do, hammer them! They said they hadn't meant it literally!

When he left school Ken worked in a factory for a while with Ron, after work he and some of the family would entertain in local venues with their skiffle group.

Ken and his first wife Jean McMahon worked in the same factory and they married in 1962. Jean was born in 1943 in Stoke Newington. They had no children and Ken and Jean later divorced.

Music took over his life and he gave up his day job after a while to work in the entertainment industry. Ken was a musician and music was his life. He sang and played guitar at pubs, clubs and dance halls across the UK until his agent found him work on US military bases in

Europe, entertaining in American NCO (non-commissioned officers) clubs for many years. As well the UK and other countries, Ken entertained in Italy, Greece and Turkey.

After meeting and marrying his wife Roula in Athens, Greece, he based himself there in Roula's home city. Ken and Roula married in February 1972. They visited England on occasion to see his mother and his family and whilst in the UK he entertained at various venues. He was a respected musician, guitarist and singer and made his living doing what he loved to do.

Sometime after the US bases were closed in Greece Ken worked for a time in a factory for Roula's father but he couldn't settle to this life, it wasn't music.

In later years he moved to the Greek island of Rhodes and entertained with both English and Greek music in a local restaurant/bar called the Pegasus. Ken was well known on the island. According to his brother Ron who visited him for holidays, everyone around the town knew and respected him.

Ken passed away on the island of Rhodes, Greece, in December 2008, aged sixty-six, the same age at which his father passed. Ken was buried in the cemetery near his home in Maritsa on Rhodes. A memorial service was held for Ken at a church in Tottenham as the families were unable to go out to Rhodes.

Ken in the middle of the back row

Sidney and Emily visiting Ken while he performed at the Blackpool Tower

Ken and Roula on their wedding day and Ken performing on stage in Rhodes

Raymond Douglas (Cod) was born in 1943. When he was an adult most of the family called him Ray. However, from a young age, his brothers nicknamed him 'Cod Eyes'. This was, Jim said, because when he was young he looked just like a cod fish because he had very large, dark eyes and so Ray became known as 'Cod Eyes', abbreviated to 'Cod'. When I was young and visited Nan Emily, I do remember many of the family still calling him Cod even as an adult. Ray didn't mind, he was a good sport and all the children grew up with the saying that most of us did years ago 'sticks and stones may hurt your bones but names can never hurt you'. If anyone was called names, it was just ignored, it meant nothing and wasn't anything to get upset about. And so it was for Ray, it was just a nickname for him.

Ray did a number of jobs when he was younger, he was a coalman and a painter and decorator. A coalman's job involved lifting 112 lbs (51kg) sacks of coal from the lorry and carrying it through the house to the coal bunker, usually located in the garden. It would then be brought into the house in a coal scuttle that sat beside the fireplace (usually a plain or decorated metal bucket, sometimes made of brass).

In later years he worked as a plumbing and heating engineer with his brother in law Frank Saville in his business.

Ray liked telling jokes and playing tricks on his

nieces and nephews whenever they visited, he also played innocent tricks on his mother too. Most of the time she knew what Ray was up to and didn't fall for his tricks. When his brother Ken was home on a visit from Greece, Ray for a joke, put a plastic fly in his sandwich before he gave it to him. We watched and waited for him to find it, he didn't and ate it! It was only small so it didn't do him any harm. We all watched in amazement as he ate the sandwich and roared with laughter afterwards. Ray, like his dad, would show us how to do tricks with playing cards.

Ray was always cheerful with a ready wit. He often took home unusual items and one that many will remember well was the full size, working jukebox. I'm not quite sure how he managed to get that jukebox up three flights of stairs to his mum's maisonette above the shops at High Cross Road. Ray remained at home until his marriage in 1976.

Ray as far as I know didn't bet on the horses or dogs, possibly the only one of the brothers that didn't. Ray did though enjoy a game of darts and cards and liked to go fishing in the River Lea in Tottenham.

When Ray was in his thirties he met Brenda Turner and they married in London in August 1976. Brenda was born at the end of the war in August 1945. Ray and Brenda lived in Croydon and Herne Hill, London. They didn't have any children but they both liked dogs and had a German Shepherd dog called Sheba. Ray used to tease Sheba too! Ray and Brenda would visit Barbara and Frank to play cards each week.

Just a few months after his brother Bill passed away, and at the same age as his paternal grandfather Herman, Ray passed away on 1st July 1999, aged just fifty-five.

Ray

Ray and Brenda

Barbara Hepting, Brenda, Barbara, Frank and Ray

Bernard Alexander (Monty) was born in 1945. Monty was named after Field Marshal Bernard Montgomery and given his 'nickname' too! Montgomery was a prominent army officer in the second world war. Monty married June Rose Foote in 1966. June was born in 1947. They had three sons. Monty and June later divorced and Monty then shared his mother's maisonette at High Cross Road, later moving with her to the house in Hanover Road, Tottenham.

June remarried in 1978.

In 1985 Monty remarried to Mary Warren, they didn't have children and later divorced. Monty, when he could, went to Greece and Rhodes on holidays to visit his brother Ken and sister in law Roula.

Monty was a postman during his working life but was also a very accomplished artist, his pencil portraits were exceptional. He could have had a career as an artist if he'd had the opportunity. Monty also liked to have a bet and always hoped for the big win, unfortunately, as for most, it never came. Monty was always cheerful, enjoyed a joke and a good laugh and would help anyone.

Monty passed away peacefully at home in Tottenham on 3rd August 2018 aged seventy-three.

Monty

Monty's ex-wife June
and mother of their three sons

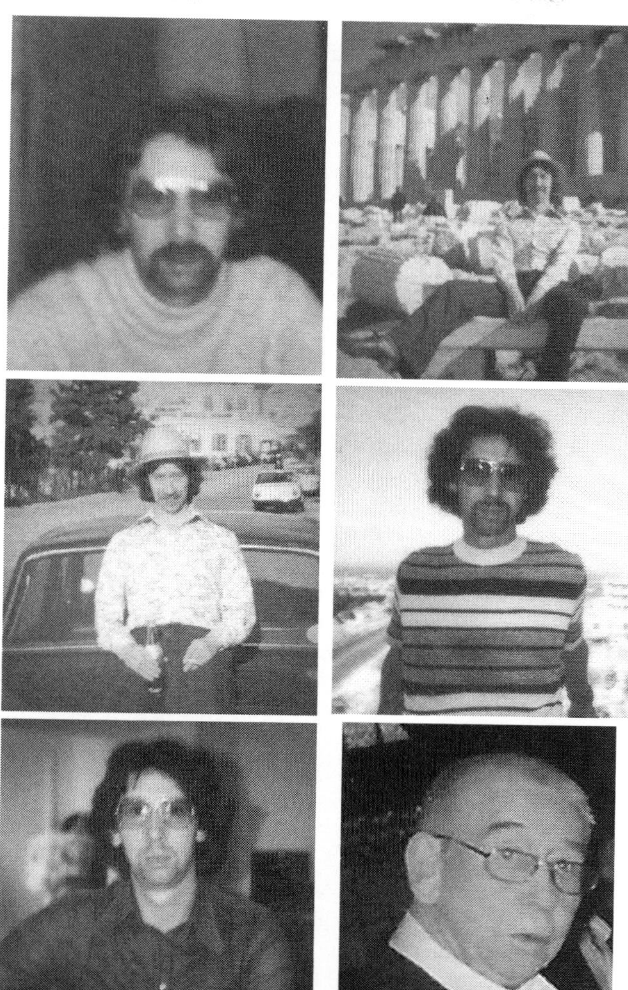

Marlene Patricia, the fourteenth child, was born on 5th February 1950 and died on 6th March 1950, surviving just one month. This must have been very hard for Emily and Sidney, after successfully bringing thirteen children into the world and then to sadly lose the fourteenth.

The Hepting Family of the Black Forest

Hepting families from our direct ancestors in the Black Forest now live throughout the UK.

On publication of this book in 2021 only Sylvie remains of the fourteen children of Emily and Sidney Hepting. Their marriage produced many children, grandchildren, great-grandchildren and great-great-grandchildren to date and the family continues to thrive.

Our ancestors left their mark on the lives of their descendants and we in turn will leave our mark on future generations. We all experience good and bad times but we can look to the past and draw strength from knowing that we have inherited the fortitude and strength of our ancestors. They overcame, survived and flourished despite the losses, pain, suffering, famine, poverty, prejudice, wars and diseases of their times.

We are but one small branch of a very large tree that is the Hepting family originating in the Black Forest region of Germany. Many others who were related to our ancestors in the Black Forest now live all around the world.

I hope the information contained within this book will serve to encourage future generations to maintain family links and to remember their origins and their ancestors.

Family Photographs

Barbara (Hepting) and husband Frank on their Golden Wedding Anniversary

Sylvie, Barbara, Monty and Beryl

Ken, Sidney, Emily and other band member

Barbara and Frank Saville's Wedding

Barbara, Frank and Ray

Emily and Roula

Emily, Ken, Roula and Roula's parents Georgios and Despina

Barbara, Sylvie, Ray, Brenda, Monty and Ron

Sylvie, Ron, George, Beryl, Barbara and Emily

Emily, Sidney, Barbara and Sylvie

Sissy, Barbara & Iris (Frank Saville's sister)

Janet (Sidney's sister) and Emily

Monty, Ken and Emily

Ken and Monty

Ken and Monty

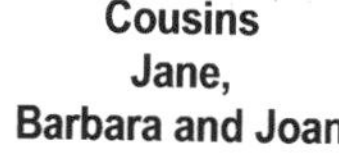

Cousins
Jane,
Barbara and Joan

Emily with son Monty

Monty, Roula and Ken

Emily with son Sidney

Sylvie and Ken

Frank and Jim

Emily Adelaide
and
Barbara (Hepting) Saville

Wally, Bill
Jim and Ray

Monty
and
Barbara (Hepting) Saville

Left to right

Stanley Rayner and his wife Joan (Sewell),
Janet Sewell
Janet (Hepting) Sewell and husband Frederick Sewell
in 1963

Kate and son Frank with dog Peter

Janet (Hepting) Sewell

Barbara and Barbara

Ron, Jim and Monty

Original Cuckoo clock made by Fidel Hepting

This photo is of an original cuckoo clock made and signed by Fidel Hepting, a well-known clockmaker in the Black Forest. Jim Hepting's eldest son now owns the clock. No family link between Anton Hepting and Fidel has been established but all those of the Hepting name in that region were family of one generation or another. It is then most likely that Fidel is related to our own lineage, assuming Lorenz Hepting to be the father of Anton Hepting!

Family Memories

Over the years family members, particularly Jim Hepting, have sent me many stories and memories about the family that they were happy to have included in this book. These memories begin with the article written by Jim Hepting called 'Home from Home'. The BBC had requested stories from anyone who remembers growing up during the second world war. Jim wrote his story and it was published by the BBC on their website. Jim also sent it to me for inclusion into this book. The story offers real insight into what life must have been like growing up in London during the war.

The stories below are all extracts from emails and letters sent to me by family members and are in their own words. Memories from some of the family members follow this article written by Jim Hepting.

Home From Home

The story of one child's experience of the Blitz and finally evacuation during the second world war.

My name is Jim. I was one of a family of 14 children, all born between 1923 and 1950. I was born in January 1934 and attended my first infants school in 1939. After attending there for a year I began to hear rumours from some of the teachers that we may all be evacuated at some stage, as a direct result of the declaration of war with Germany. Just before I was about to leave the school one afternoon I saw a big lorry drive up to the main gate. There were men on the back of the lorry in uniform, women also. They unloaded a massive silvery looking object into the playground. When we all arrived at school the following morning we were amazed to see a large silver balloon floating above the school.

It was our first sight of what we later found out to be a barrage balloon, a defence against the German airplanes that were expected to carry out air raids on London.

We all stood gazing at this massive balloon which was going to be a permanent feature in our playground, at least until it was sent soaring high into the sky with its thick wire cables holding it to the ground. It had three half round tail pieces on the back which were keeping it in one place. On the ground it was being controlled by several people, including women, all in uniform. One day while we were all sitting in the classroom there was an almighty crash on the school roof as the balloon had blown out of control as it was being lowered in a strong wind.

We all thought that a bomb had hit the school, as there were tiles and pieces of stonework all falling into the playground. I have never heard such a loud noise. I never felt too safe at all after that incident. The school was Stamford Hill infant and junior school, Seven Sisters Road, Tottenham. That incident may well still be on record in the local town hall archives.

One Monday morning when we were all in the assembly hall, our headmaster Mr Crab informed us all that we may all have to be evacuated to the countryside if it was considered that London would be a main target for the Luftwaffe, the German air force.

Months passed and there was no sign of German planes. My father had joined up as an Air Raid Warden, and my eldest brother Sid joined up at 17 years of age into the Army and after training went into the Airborne division. Another brother, Bill, joined the Merchant Navy. They both looked very smart in their uniforms and

I used to look forward to them coming home on leave. My father's warden post was not far from our house and my mother used to take him some sandwiches and a jug of tea when he was on duty. I used to go and see him quite regularly. He was always playing cards with his other warden friends.

Everything remained peaceful and quiet for the next few months. It was difficult to believe that we were at war at all. Then, one day, as we all sat at our desks in the school classroom we heard the air raid warning siren begin to wail. We had heard it before, mainly when they were testing and practising in the event of an air raid.

This was for real, we all heard the intermittent drone of the German bombers high overhead on this particular day and the teachers herded us all into a concrete air raid shelter in the corner of the girl's playground. We sat in there and just listened. There seemed to be many bombers in the sky, but our school barrage balloon was not high enough at that stage to do any real harm. I will never forget the noise of those German planes, but fortunately all of their bombs fell pretty wide of our school. We could hear the strange whistle as the bombs screamed earthwards, then there came the explosions in the distance. this went on for approximately half an hour before we heard the sound of the all clear. That raid made me really frightened that day.

On the same night we were all indoors keeping ourselves amused listening to a speech by Adolf Hitler, on an old Cossor radio that had a very large battery in the back and an accumulator. I never knew what the accumulator did or what purpose it served. The radio was quite crackly but we all listened to the ranting and raving of this German, who they called the Fuhrer.

On this same night the air raid warning sounded again and after about five minutes we heard the dreaded drone of the German planes again. This was now about 10 o'clock at night and my mother rushed us all out into the back garden and into an Anderson air raid shelter made of corrugated iron. It was half buried in earth and was right at the back of the garden. Everybody had them delivered months before the air raids, but we never really expected to have to use them. Being such a big family we couldn't all get in, so the neighbours either side of us lifted some of us over their fences and we stayed in their shelters until the all clear sounded.

The night raid was more frightening to me as a child because I hated the dark anyway, and we could not have any form of light on because of the blackout rules. It was pitch black, cold and wet in our shelter.

Then all of a sudden there was a massive explosion which sounded very near, the ground shook, and you could hear lumps of metal hitting the roofs of the nearby houses. It was shrapnel, fragments of the bombs flying everywhere as they exploded. All of a sudden my old mum started singing, and one of my brothers played the mouth organ, and we finished up a lot more cheerful then. The bombs just kept exploding everywhere and you could see the sky light up with an orange, red glow as the buildings and factories went up in flames. This went on night after night, after the initial daylight raids, so my mum decided that next time a night raid came we would get to the Manor House underground station as it was safer there. We arrived there carrying old blankets and sheets and made our way down to the station platform.

I will always remember those people already down there just lying around on makeshift beds. One man was playing a piano accordion and many of them were singing along with him. People of all ages and all backgrounds all joined in together. I recall lying awake all night wondering if a bomb was going to fall and bury us all alive. That was my biggest fear down the underground. During the day all the kids would be out searching for pieces of shrapnel from the bombs and anti-aircraft shells that were fired at the German planes all throughout the raid. But the shells were a waste of time because the planes were too high to hit. Barrage balloons were flying everywhere. The whole sky was covered with them.

My mother had now had enough of London and the terrible danger of remaining there during these raids so she finally decided that we would all be evacuated. I was sent to Cornwall, a little village named Goonhavern, where I lived with a very nice family, named Eplett. My mother went with the youngest children to Luton in Bedfordshire. My father stayed in London, as he had a job to do as an air raid warden. In fact we were scattered all over the country. Two in Norfolk, another two in South Wales.

In late 1944, just before the war ended I returned to London. A V2 rocket had decimated a whole area of the road I lived in, Tewkesbury Road in Tottenham. My mother lost two of her best friends when a flying bomb had fallen on Broadwater Road, Tottenham. It is now the site of the Broadwater Farm Estate. As I looked around at the bomb sites all over the place I was glad we had been evacuated from the worst of the Blitz.

Our own house had every pane of glass smashed out due to the rocket blast but they had been boarded up until the war damage companies got round to repairing everything. My Dad told me he had slept in the warden's post most nights when it was quiet. When all the family were re-united at the end of the war we all felt like strangers to each other as we had been split up for so long. I am glad to say we all finished up safe and sound. Ours was a happy story, although it did take us all some time to re-adjust to our virtual slum surroundings after living in more comfortable homes during evacuation.

Memories from Jim Hepting

The dog board

Yes, the good old days. We played dogs every Saturday night. It was a ritual. Your dad Bill and I used to pair up as partners so we had two chances of winning. We shared anything we won. Frank Anthony John Herman, what a mouthful, used to bring his little son Ronnie to play. Ronnie was really blonde and we all used to comment on how he looked like a typical member of the Nazi youth! If brother Siddy's dog got beat on the run in, the air turned blue and my mum used to say, 'alright Sid, there's no need for that language'. It was a bundle of laughs then. The whole room was filled with cigarette smoke, you could hardly see each other. Then, if young Ronnie's dog was in front he used to stand up at the table in excitement and keep repeating in a long voice, 'That's my dog daddy, that's my dog daddy' to uncle Frank. Then came the grand finale, about 2'o'clock in the morning, everyone put five shillings in the pool for the last race. The winner took all, about £3. Nowadays I lose that in the lining of my pockets.

If my dad had a bad night and had consistently lost on the dog board you could guarantee he would challenge someone to a game of draughts before the session ended. Uncle Frank fell for it every time, and some of the younger members of the family, including myself. The two players would put two shillings in each. My dad would finish up with a pocketful of two shilling pieces before everyone left to go home. I have got my own dog board now. We have a few games at xmas, the grandchildren love it. When they are playing, and arguing, they don't know the memories that brings back to me. The only difference is, I won't let the kids play for money.

Memories of mum, dad and nan

Yes, my old mum could tell a good story about her past. Her mother Emily Elizabeth Hearn was born in Ireland to Mary Ann (Nunn) Hearn. Her father, John Hearn was a glass cutter. It may sound strange to you but I can remember Emily Hearn, my grandmother, lying on a single bed in our front room at Tewkesbury Road, very ill. She eventually died in April 1934, aged 69 years. I was three months old then, as I was born in January 1934. It goes to prove that the memory is quite retentive, even from such a young age. The one thing I do remember the most was a very sweet, sickly smell in that room, probably the smell of death, but I was not aware that she was dying. It's really weird because sometimes I have to struggle to remember something that happened six months ago. My old dad had a theory that when a new child is born, someone has just died in another life and another age, and the new born child is a replacement of that other person, in soul and spirit. That's how he accounted for people resembling someone else from the past, as he considered that only the body dies but the spirit and soul lives on by an automatic transmission to a new born baby. He always used to say that we had all lived in a previous life somewhere on the planet. I'm not sure that I could subscribe to that theory, but it's an interesting subject.

Mum was in service when a girl

I do know she was in service as a domestic servant. It was possibly in the Stamford Hill area as she worked for a Jewish family for a long time. She told me they treated her very well and gave her 5 shillings a day, she was about 16 then I believe round about 1920, not bad for those days. But it all came to a bad end when the man of the house tried to kiss her while she was making the bed in the main bedroom. Knowing how straight laced my mum was, that was the end of a good friendship and a well-paid job. She just left and never went back. In 1923, at 18, she married my dad, Sid. That was the beginning of the Hepting clan in Tottenham.

Grandad Bedford

Yes, my old mum was straight to the point and scrupulously fair with everyone. She had good principles. They came from her father Robert R Bedford. He was a strict disciplinarian. One of the military school. We nicknamed him Teddy Bear Picnic. That originated from years before I was born. Someone in the family complained to him that there were too many jobs to do around the house on a Saturday, and he shouted at them 'What do ya think this is then on a Saturday, a bloody teddy bear's picnic'. That stuck and he got the nickname. I remember him well, very stern, unemotional, unfeeling type. He loved to control people. That stemmed from his many years in the Army in India. He was the original 'OLD GIT' from the Harry Enfield shows.

I broke up a load of brown top matches when I was about 10 years of age and I crunched them up and put the powder in his tobacco box. He smoked Boar's Head, dark, strong tobacco. When he rolled his next cigarette it went up like a roman candle. He went ballistic and told my mum that we should all be put in a home as were out of control but lucky for me he never knew who tampered with his tobacco. He had to throw the remainder away. He knew what had been done to it though, you could smell the match top powder. I have never seen anything so funny. It was just like he had a firework in his mouth, did he get rid of that roll up quick, and the language, it would have made the devil blush.

A night at the races

I can remember your dad and myself going to Haringey dog track in the 1950s with our last £2. It was a week before xmas and we had to get some cash somehow. I left the betting to your dad. Luck was with us on that night. Bill backed three winners on the run and in the last race we were about £22 up. I nearly died when he said to me, 'we'll stick the lot on number 6 in this race. I reluctantly agreed, with thoughts of a miserable xmas. I couldn't watch the race so I went to the toilet with my fingers crossed. I came back after the shouting had died down and half covering my eyes with my hand I looked at the results board and there it was. Winner, number 6. Price 11 to 4. It was the greatest feeling I can ever remember. Your mum would probably remember that night, as we went back to her place and walked in looking really glum, pretending we had come back broke. Then your dad Bill pulled out a wad of notes and threw them up in the air. Luvvly Jubbly. We must have had a guardian angel that xmas. We had about £60 each. Millionaires. What a xmas!

Louisa Frances Hepting

Anton's son Anthony William was known as Bill Hepting according to Anton's granddaughter, Louisa Frances, Albert Mark's daughter, who I visited in 1995 in Marylebone, she was 91 then and has since died. She gave me quite a lot of information about Anton and his family. He was a strict disciplinarian and she told me that they were all in awe of him in his later life. He was in partnership in Oxford Street, with a German clockmaker named Marz pronounced Marts. It was called Hepting and Marz. There was a large street clock hanging in Oxford Street with their name on it. It hung over an establishment named Mooney's. (sounds like a nightclub or gambling casino). She also told me that Anton would sit all evening with his eyeglasses on and a little black round hat mending clocks and watches in their drawing room at 37 Newman Street.

Raymond and the Oxford Street clock

Raymond remembers seeing the clock years ago when he was shopping in Oxford Street but he didn't pay much attention to it. He was young then but did mention it to us when he got back home. My dad didn't even know that it was his grandfather's clock Raymond was talking about. Not his grandfather clock, his grandfather's clock, there is a difference, ha ha.

Learning German

Brother Siddy could speak German quite well and we used to write in German to each other as a method of learning. I picked up quite a lot by doing that. I then bought a couple of basic German language books which I read over and over again. Once I had got the gist of the language, not advanced German, that is a four year course. I then bought a book on Old German script so that I could decipher the information from the archives.

It's only our family history that has given me an interest in the language. Anthony Hepting, Siddy's adopted son, married a German girl and can speak and write perfect German. She wrote a couple of letters for us in the beginning, very nice girl.

Our mum Emily

Mum had brothers and sisters. To me they were Aunt Nan, Uncle Bob (Robert) and Uncle Jack (John), he served in the Black and Tans regiment in Northern Ireland. When he left the Army he was always fighting someone, mostly in the local pubs. Uncle George was a brilliant artist. I saw some of his pictures of battle scenes of the Crimean war. He had one hanging in a London gallery, not sure which one though. His daughter Florrie (Florence) lived in Walthamstow for many years. I used to see her up the market sometimes. She died not too long ago.

The doodlebug in Tewkesbury Road

The doodlebug was an awesome sight. I remember it well. Leslie and I were out playing in the street when we heard this noise of an aeroplane in the sky. When we looked up we saw this doodlebug, pilotless plane, all of a sudden the engine cut out right above Tewkesbury Road. Les and I ran for our street door and pulled the string to get in. Mum came flying up the passage and there was a terrible explosion. All the windows caved in with glass flying everywhere. The street door was blasted off its hinges and it caught mum in the chest, knocking her flying.

My dad was in the Air Raid Warden's post and came running home to see if we were ok. Bill was working in a laundry in Tewkesbury Road when the doodlebug fell and he dropped everything and flew home.

A relation of ours was killed outright in Tewkesbury and friends of mum's, a whole family, perished. It was an awesome sight, people running with blood pouring from their injuries, ambulances and police all over the place. Lucky for us the doodlebug glided for a while before it actually crashed to earth.

The next day we were all down on the bomb site playing amongst the rubble and jumping in the massive crater which had filled with water from burst mains pipes. A ready-made swimming pool for us kids. Years later mum had a lump appear in the breast that took the blow from the street door. That must have been the cause of the cancer. The following Sunday another flying bomb streaked over Tewkesbury Road and landed in Broadwater Road. It demolished streets and houses and it eventually was rebuilt as Broadwater Farm Estate.

Mum and Dad's visits to Kate and Herman

Mum and Dad used to visit Herman and Kate every Saturday and played cards and draughts. I have never seen anyone beat my dad at draughts. He was the Kasparov of the draught board. He used to play for money and Herman must have lost a fortune over the years trying to beat my dad. Kate was not German, she came from Shaftesbury in Dorset. They call that Hardy country. Thomas Hardy also came from Dorset. Auntie Lou, Herman's sister was a rank German looking fräulein. She was a real blonde and had a long plait hanging down the back of her hair. Full name, Louisa Christina and she is listed on the 1881 census at 37 Newman Street, Marylebone. Kate Florence Hardy did used to have buns in her hair and you could have taken her for a typical German woman if you didn't know her history. She was also a wicked liar. On her marriage certificate she gave her age as twenty-six but if you work out her age from when she was born in 1866, in 1901 when she married she would have been thirty-five. How she got away with that I'll never know because Herman was only twenty.

My lucky pixie

Years ago when we played dogs all night at our house at Station Road, Tottenham Hale, I can recall I had a really lucky Saturday night and had won about four races on the turn with my little cardboard, trap two greyhound. I also had my lucky Cornish pixie on the table beside me. My dad hadn't won a race or a forecast nearly all night and I kept rubbing my lucky pixie before every race and by magic it worked for me that particular night. That's the power of positive thought.

On the very last race there was a forecast pool of about £4 that had built up and I started working on my pixie before the race started. Believe it or not I won the big forecast with 2-3. Couldn't stop throwing sixes on the dice and my dad's dog was well behind on the dog-board, about 4th and as I scooped in my winnings he said, in true Hepting fashion, "fuck your pixie" and he then brushed it off the table with his hand and knocked it flying across the room. He was so wound up because he had been losing all night, and me winning the final race forecast triggered him off. I've never laughed so much in my life. I still giggle when I think about it even now. I had tears in my eyes after his outburst, plus the smoke from about ten people all puffing during the game. First time I'd seen a pixie attacked by a human.

Monty, who was very young at the time, still remembers

it and often reminds me when we talk about the old days. He saw the funny side of it too. I still have the pixie. I wouldn't be without it because it reminds me of the past each time I look at it.

Every time we started a dog game I placed my pixie on the table next to me and dad used to try and put a curse on it by looking at it and saying "nichts, nichts", words he picked up from his dad Herman, years before he married our Mum. In German it meant "nothing, nothing"... meaning that he had cursed it and I would win nothing. But I always did. Siddy used to nearly fall off the chair laughing. It was all in good fun though.

The old Cossor radio

Another funny incident was when mum was talking to a neighbour, Mrs Whelan, in the kitchen at Station Road and dad was trying to listen to something on the radio, a big old Cossor valve radio that weighed a ton and he kept turning it up louder to drown out their voices. It was bedlam, and impossible to continue the conversation, so as soon as the neighbour went, mum turned round and said to dad, "why don't you hang that fucking wireless on your earhole". Mum only ever swore on rare occasions, and that was one of them.

Tricksters and jokers

One of dad's favourites, when we were gullible kids, was to wet a sixpence and press it on his forehead. He would then shake his head until it fell off. With us lined up he then pressed what we thought was a sixpence on our foreheads. Then told us to repeat what he did and we'd be shaking our heads like mad but no coin came off. There was never any coin to come off, he would roll up laughing at that one. There would be about five of us all shaking our heads – wicked sod, ha ha ha. Never really saw him miserable. He just loved little jokes and tricks and kept us kids amused for hours.

His dad, Herman was the same, loved mending our toys and showing us little tricks and games when we were very young. I was only three years old when he died but remember him well. He always wore a collarless pinstripe shirt with braces and a big, buckled leather belt and black boots, a bit like Alf Garnett. He was on the plump side, our Frank looked very much like him.

Family of musicians

It was noisy at our house, especially when Ray, Ronnie and Ginger used to rehearse music playing their guitars in the front room at home. Our dad was on drums, he loved it, as old as he was. The only instrument I can play is a comb with a piece of tissue paper. Your dad Bill was a great Harmonica player. He could play anything and he loved the Inkspots. Whispering Grass was his favourite. When he used to sing it sounded just like the Inkspots record but without the music.

A nightmare or something else?

Some years ago some days after my dad died I had a real life like dream about him. It was so real it was frightening.

I was asleep in our back bedroom upstairs at Alexandra Road, Walthamstow. It was in the early hours when I was woken up by a constant tapping on the window of the bedroom. I sat bolt upright and looked straight at the window which had rain pouring down the glass. Outside was the image of dad, no ladder, nothing, but he was at window level about 15 feet up the wall. He was looking in, absolutely drenched to the skin and looking very pale and drawn, with hollow eyes. I couldn't fathom out for a minute whether I was still dreaming or actually awake, or half and half. He obviously was tapping on the window to tell me something, so I thought in my semi nightmare. I remember saying, dad, what do you want, you're dead? He looked at me, and it all seemed so real, and said, "tell mum I'm not dead, I'm still alive".......with that he was gone and I now was fully awake and not feeling too comfortable either because I have never believed in ghosts or the paranormal. I can only say that if it was a dream it's the most realistic one I can ever recall happening to me...but why?

The day before he died, Frank Saville, Barbara's husband, phoned me up and said I ought to get over to my mum's place at High Cross as the doctor told those at home that he wasn't going to last the week out. He was on a high dosage of morphine at the time, so I rushed over there that night. I went up to his sick bed and he was lying there looking absolutely dreadful, hollow cheeks and eye sockets, thin and bony and looking quite whitish and yellowish. It was all he could do to raise himself up slightly and in a very weak voice, not far from a whisper, he said Hello Jim, can you ask mum to come up. So I called down to Mum to come up as he said he wanted a glass of water. I left about an hour later as he was still alive, but barely, drifting in and out of consciousness. I thought he might last for another day or two but he died the next day.

The face I saw in that dream was the exact face he had when I visited him that night, and I believe it stayed in my subconscious so indelibly that it prompted the dream I had. Why couldn't I have dreamed of him in his normal healthy state which I had known for years, since

I was a kid? The strangest thing was, it was actually raining that night I had the dream and he was soaked. That made the dream more real.

It's not a dream I would like to repeat.

From Farmer to Clockmaker

How do you go from farmer to clockmaker? The transition must have been over many decades. You don't learn a skill like that overnight. Talking about clocks, my cuckoo clock stopped ticking today, just before noon. I have had it to pieces tonight and dusted it out with a small sable paint brush, sprayed some WD40 in the back and it's ticking away merrily again. The craftsmanship in the hand carving is out of this world.

Every time I look at my cuckoo clock it takes me on a trip to the Black Forest of that period. I try to picture them in their little workshops, beavering away while their wives are out in the forest collecting more wood for the next batch of clocks. I read a book on the Uhrmachers (Clockmakers) of the Black Forest and it explained that, the wives of the farmers collected the fallen wood in the forest initially to burn on their open hearth fires. Then, during early bad winter months, when heavy snow prevented any farming of the fields they started to collect more wood to carve the cases for the local clockmakers who bought them from them. Initially they were not clockmakers themselves, just hand carvers. The farmers then began to learn to make the actual clocks in the clockmaking apprentice school in Furtwangen which later became a factory for mass producing the clocks.

Franz Ketterer was the first clockmaker to produce the cuckoo sound by using bellows. Furtwangen eventually became the main clockmaking town in the

Schwarzwald (Black Forest). From Germany the clockmaking trade spread to Switzerland.

Memories from Barbara (Hepting) Saville

A family wedding party ends with a punch up!

At a family wedding there was a band playing. Towards the end of the evening Jim, Siddy and Bill wanted to get up and sing a song using the microphone, the band got stroppy with them and one of them said to Bill, I've got a brown belt in Judo. Bill punched him and said, now you've got a black eye to go with it, all hell let loose in the hall and the band left without being paid. They should have known not to upset the Hepting family.

Four of us married in 1959, Beryl and Ron in March, me in July and Sylvie in December.

Memories of growing up in Tottenham

I was born in 1938 in Tewkesbury Road,Tottenham. I attended Stamford Hill School, in Seven Sisters Road. I remember they used to have a Barrage Balloon in the playground and we often had to seek shelter whilst the war was on.

At the weekend a man used to come round with his barrow selling cockles and winkles which we always had for tea on a Sunday. We also had a man come round with a horse and cart, the cart was like a roundabout and we used to pay him a penny or a clean jam jar for a ride to the bottom of the road and back.

In 1946 at the age of eight years we moved to Station Road, Tottenham Hale. I had nine brothers and four sisters, some of us attended Down Lane Junior school, sat the 11 plus and then went to Page Green School (which was demolished for new flats to be built) opposite the print company, Gestetners, in Broad Lane. I left school in 1953 and worked at the Ever Ready factory in Ashley Road, from there I went to work at Dickinsons, a few years later I worked at the Mills Equipment in Fountayne Road, from there I left to get married at the age of twenty-one.

My memories of those days were the Municipal Baths, The Royal Tottenham, the Corner Picture House, the Palace at Bruce Grove, the Florida and the Imperial cinemas. The pubs I remember although I didn't frequent them were the White Hart, the Hope and Anchor, the Volunteer and the Beehive. Upstairs in the Beehive my fiancé, Frank and I used to go to learn Ballroom Dancing. We used to go to the Lido swimming pool during the summer.

Christmas in our house was always chaos with all my brothers and sisters thoroughly enjoying themselves, but my parents struggled to bring us all up and they used to hire out a barrow and go round the streets selling celery and all sorts of vegetables to earn a few coppers to put food on the table for us all. We didn't have a lot but we enjoyed what little we did have. Tottenham has changed a lot since those days and I feel very sad that a lot of our buildings that we loved have been destroyed, the Prince of Wales Hospital, the large Post Office in the High Cross, and all the cinemas previously mentioned here. Tottenham Hale itself, where I used to live in Station Road, is just not recognisable any more.

Mum and dad first met

Mum met my dad on Monkey's Parade, Tottenham High Road. Apparently dad used to draw in a crowd of people watching him step dancing (tap dancing I would have called it). Monkeys Parade, was at the bottom end of West Green Road, on the corner where Rudd's store was, I believe it was used as a speakers corner and I remember my dad used to go and listen to some of them. I think they were called the black shirts.

A note on Monkey's Parade

It's possible that this area of Tottenham was known as Monkey's Parade but the term 'Monkey's Parade' was a term used in the early 1900's to describe the practice of young men parading in their best clothes on a Sunday to attract the young ladies. This usually took place in parks or along a local street.

Dad's tricks

Yes he was always playing tricks on us as kids, he used to keep us amused. He also sent me to the shops to get 'spotted paint', he was always up to something.

When dad used to go out anywhere special, he used to get his tin of shoe black, dip a matchstick in it and pencil his moustache in to make it blacker. Another one was to get a bit of lard and mum's perfume rub both in his hands together and then put it on his hair he was up to all sorts of tricks.

Mum's family

Her family came from Offaly in Ireland, her mother was one of a triplet, of which one died, their surname was Hearn or Hearne. I didn't know my grandmother, I think she must have died before I was born.

A ghostly experience

Grandad (Picnic) Bedford, said that he went to bed one night, and tapped his pipe out on the table at the side and saw a vision of a woman in long flowing gown, he said he tapped his pipe again to make sure he wasn't dreaming. In the Woodberry pub the next day he was telling one of his mates, his mate said, we did hear a story of a woman dressed that way there, she fell down the stairs in that house and broke her neck and died.

Raymond and the Jellied eels

I remember one time Raymond bought some jellied eels in and had to reach over my dad to get to the cutlery drawer to get a fork and as he did so the carton tilted and the eels dropped into dad's jacket pocket and left Raymond with an empty carton we all had a laugh over that.

The Suspender Belt

I found that Beryl was borrowing my clothes without my permission, so I bought a very large suit case and asked Frank to put a couple of very large padlocks on it, so that she couldn't get to them. One day I was looking for my suspender belt and I went home to dinner, mum always cooked a midday meal and I was with Frank at the time. Beryl was there and Frank said 'Beryl get Barbara's suspender belt off' because I had already told Frank that I thought she had it, (This was before the padlocks went on) my mum was fuming I could tell by the expression on her face. She didn't say anything at the time but when I came home in the evening and Frank had gone home to his house, mum said, 'why did Frank mention your underwear' and she gave me such a walloping, you wasn't supposed to mention unmentionables with my mum she was very narrow minded. I could have killed Beryl, if she hadn't taken my clothes in the first place the row wouldn't have occurred. Frank couldn't understand it when I told him as his parents weren't at all strict, I have to laugh now.

'Using his loaf'

Sid and Leslie pinched a loaf of bread that was cooling on the window sill of the bakery near their home when they were kids. Leslie was on the road keeping an eye out and he shouted out, copper coming. Sid having the loaf in his hand threw it at the copper, it knocked off his helmet but he managed to catch Sid. Apparently the policeman said to them if I knew you were hungry I would have given you a couple of bob. That story really made me laugh.

(Jim told the same story but seemed to think that it did end up in the court and the final remark of the magistrate to Sid was 'At least you used your loaf'!)

Memories from
Sylvia (nee Hepting) (Pickley) Kelly

Grandparents

I don't remember my mum's parents, I can't remember ever being taken to their house. I do remember my sister, Barbara, telling me about grandad Bedford. Barbara told me that mum had taken her to visit her grandad Bedford and she was sitting on the stairs with her hands resting on them. Grandad Bedford trod on her hands and mum had words with him because he was ranting about Barbara being in his way. He was apparently known for being a grumpy old man. Mum used to talk about him being very strict and hard in his manner and how he was always right. I only met one grandparent and that was Kate, my dad's mum, she lived in Edmonton. I was taken to visit her and cats appeared from everywhere in her house, there must have been about eight, she loved cats.

Brother Bill (Stanley Victor)

Bill was always up to mischief when he was young. He asked me to go to the coal cellar to get some coal for the fire. I shouted out that there was no light, he said, 'I'll come and fix it.' He came to the cellar with a fork in his hand and was messing around with some loose wires. He asked me to touch the wires with the fork and I complied as asked, it gave me an electric shock right up my arm! I then warned my other brothers and sisters not to be caught out like I was. I always laughed about it afterwards but at the time it made me jump out of my skin.

Memories from Frank and Vilma's daughter

Barbara and Bill Hepting's sons

I do remember when we used to go to the pub (City Arms) we would pop round the corner and get a bag of chips, we tipped the vinegar bottle to put over the chips and the whole bloody bottle of vinegar would pour out, we looked round and it was one of your brothers giggling, it was him that had unscrewed the tops.

I remember your mum and dad with such pride, wonderful people, proud to call them my aunt and uncle.

Eight Generations Of The Hepting Family

THE FIRST GENERATION

Joseph KIRNER (1759-1835) and Justina HEITZMAN (1760-1822)
Aloysius HEPTING (1761-?) and Maria WILLMAN (1750-?)

THE SECOND GENERATION

Gertrud KIRNER (1797-18??)
Lorenz HEPTING (1790-1859)

THE THIRD GENERATION

Anton HEPTING (born KIRNER) (1819-1892)

THE FOURTH GENERATION

Justina (Hepting) JAEGGLE (1844-?)
Sophia Hepting (1846-1849)
Anton (Anthony) HEPTING (1849-1920)
Bernhard Hepting (1851-?)
Maria (Hepting) SPITZ (1853-?)
Markus Hepting (1855-1901)
Alois Hepting (1858-?)

THE FIFTH GENERATION

Anthony William Hepting (1873-1943)
Louisa Christina (Hepting) WOOLNER (1875-1964)
Albert Mark Hepting (1876-1940)
Herman Adolph Hepting (1881-1937)
Frank Sidney Hepting (1885-1903)

THE SIXTH GENERATION

Sidney William Charles Hepting (1902-1968)
Frank Anthony John Herman Hepting (1903-1979)
Janet Florence Louise (Hepting) SEWELL (1909-2002)

THE SEVENTH GENERATION

Sidney Robert Hepting (1923-2001)
Emily Margaret (Hepting) WOODROFFE (1925-2011)
Stanley Victor Hepting (1927-1999)
Frank Terence Hepting (1930-2002)
Leslie Charles Hepting (1933-2010)
James William Hepting (1934-2014)
Ronald Edward Hepting (1936-2020)
Ann Barbara (Hepting) SAVILLE (1938-2020)
Sylvia Gwendolyn (Hepting) (Pickley) KELLY (1939-)
Beryl Rosemary (Hepting) (Newson) CAMPBELL (1940-2019)
Kenneth Roy Hepting (1942-2008)
Raymond Douglas Hepting (1943-1999)
Bernard Alexander Hepting (1945-2018)
Marlene Patricia Hepting (1950-1950)

THE EIGHTH GENERATION

Sidney R Hepting (1923-2001) and Sarah J MURPHY (1933-2010)
Six children

Emily M Hepting (1925-2011) and Walter WOODROFFE (1922-2012)
Eight children

Stanley V Hepting (1927-1999) and Barbara WARD (1933-2017)
Five children

Frank T Hepting (1930-2002) and Vilma KILROW (1929-2017)
One child

James W Hepting (1934-2014) and Doreen HOLMES (1941-)
Three children

Ronald E Hepting (1936-2020) and Ruby MOLES (1940-2014)
Three children

Ann B Hepting (1938-2020) and Frank SAVILLE (1935-2012)
Three children

Sylvia G Hepting (1939-) and Thomas PICKLEY (?-?)
Two children

Sylvia G Hepting (1939-) and Michael KELLY (?-?)
One child

Beryl Rosemary Hepting (1940-2019) and George NEWSON (?-?)
Five children

Beryl Rosemary Hepting and Robert CAMPBELL (?-?)
One child

Bernard A Hepting (1945-2018) and June Rose FOOTE (1947-)
Three children

INDEX OF FAMILY MEMBERS LIVING YEARS

HEARN Mary	1862-?
HEARN Robert	1805-1872
HEARN Sarah	1864-?
HEITZMAN Justina	1760-1822
HEPTING Albert	1895-?
HEPTING Albert	1905-1909
HEPTING Albert Mark	1876-1940
HEPTING Alois	1858-?
HEPTING Aloysius	1761-?
HEPTING Andreas	1887-?
HEPTING Anna	1881-?
HEPTING Ann Barbara (Barbara)	1938-2020
HEPTING Anthony William	1873-1943
HEPTING Anton (Anthony)	1849-1920
HEPTING Anton (from 1826) (born Kirner)	1819-1892
HEPTING Antonius	1893-1893
HEPTING Bernard Alexander (Monty)	1945-2018
HEPTING Bernhard	1851-?
HEPTING Bernhard	1894-?
HEPTING Beryl Rosemary	1940-2019
HEPTING Dorothy Winifred	1909-1997
HEPTING Emily Margaret (Sissy)	1925-2011
HEPTING Frank Anthony John Herman	1903-1979
HEPTING Frank Sidney	1885-1903
HEPTING Frank Terence	1930-2002
HEPTING Harry	1911-1979
HEPTING Herman Adolph	1881-1937
HEPTING Ida	1891-?
HEPTING James William	1934-2014
HEPTING Janet Florence Louise	1909-2002
HEPTING Johannes	1891-?
HEPTING Justina	1844-?
HEPTING Karolina	1885-?
HEPTING Kenneth Roy (Ginger)	1942-2008
HEPTING Leopold	1888-?
HEPTING Leslie Charles	1933-2010
HEPTING Lorenz	1790-1859
HEPTING Louisa Christina	1875-1964
HEPTING Louisa Frances	1903-2001

HEPTING Markus (Mark)	1855-1901
HEPTING Maria	1853-?
HEPTING Maria	1878-?
HEPTING Marlene Patricia	1950-1950
HEPTING Raymond Douglas (Cod)	1943-1999
HEPTING Ronald Edward	1936-2020
HEPTING Ronald Frank	1942-2013
HEPTING Sidney Robert	1923-2001
HEPTING Sidney William Charles	1902-1968
HEPTING Sophia	1846-1849
HEPTING Stanley Victor (Bill)	1927-1999
HEPTING Sylvia (Sylvie) Gwendolyn	1939-
HEPTING Victor Bernard	1934-2002
HEPTING William Bernard	1907-1981
HETTICH Ludwina	1866-?
HOLLIS Caroline Alice	1875-1931
HOLMES Doreen	1941-
HUNT Amelia Motton	1818-1867
JAEGGLE Bernhard	1878-?
JAEGGLE Joseph	1846-?
JAEGGLE Johanna	1880-?
JAEGGLE Justina	1885-?
KILROW Vilma	1929-2017
KIRNER Agatha	1790-1858
KIRNER Gertrud	1797-?
KIRNER Gertrudis	1817-1817
KIRNER Helena	1792-1857
KIRNER Joseph	1759-1835
LETCHFORD June	1938-?
MARRIOTT Anne	?
McCULLUM Frances Isabella (Fanny)	1873-1929
McMAHON Jean	1943-?
MICHAEL Roula	?
MOLES Ruby	1940-2014
MURPHY Sarah Jane	1933-2010
NEWSON George	1936-2013
NUNN Joseph James	1807-1854
NUNN Mary Ann	1834-1897

PARSONS Mary	1811-?
PAVELIN Jean	1945-?
PICKLEY Thomas	1935-?
PROSSER Maud Kathleen	1921-1998
RAYNER Stanley	1924-2009
ROBBINS Mary Jane	1835-1924
SAUNDERS Bertie Thomas	1891-1932
SAVILLE Frank	1935-2012
SEWELL Frederick J C	1948-
SEWELL Frederick W C	1913-1966
SEWELL Janet	1950-
SEWELL Joan	1938-
SHARPLESS Robert	1805-1862
SHARPLESS Sarah Elizabeth	1834-?
SMITH Jean	1948-1896
SPITZ Amanda	1890-1890
SPITZ Anna	1893-?
SPITZ Franciscus	1886-?
SPITZ Friedrich	1883-1883
SPITZ Juditha	1885-?
SPITZ Karl	1851-?
SPITZ Karolina	1888-?
SPITZ Maria Wilhelmina	1884-?
STEPHENSON Sarah Sophia	1806-1855
SYKES Rose Adelaide	1906-1972
TRITSCHLER Maria	1853-?
TURNER Brenda	1945-
WARD Barbara Lilian	1933-2017
WARREN Mary	?
WILLMAN Maria	1750-?
WILSHER Doreen	?
WINTERHALDER Joseph	1815-?
WINTERHALDER Sophia	1849-1851
WOODROFFE Walter (Wally)	1922-2012
WOOLNER Dorothy Rose	1906-1967
WOOLNER Harry	1897-1916
WOOLNER Henry James	1873-1940
WOOLNER Norman Frank	1913-1970
WOOLNER Winifred Christine	1901-1994

INDEX OF BIRTH, MARRIAGES, DEATHS

1750 – 2020

1750	Birth of Maria Willman
1759	Birth of Joseph Kirner
1760	Birth of Justina Heitzman
1761	Birth of Aloysius Hepting
1783	Birth of Magdelena Beha
1784	Marriage of Maria Willman to Aloysius Hepting
1785	Birth of Johannes Ganter
1790	Birth of Agatha Kirner
	Birth of Lorenz Hepting
	Marriage of Justina Heitzman to Joseph Kirner
1792	Birth of Helena Kirner
1797	Birth of Gertrud Kirner
1800	Birth of Michael Brugger
1801	Birth of Johannes Baptista Haas
1805	Birth of Robert Hearn
	Birth of Robert Sharpless
1806	Birth of Sarah Sophia Stephenson
1807	Birth of Joseph James Nunn
1811	Birth of Mary Parsons
1812	Birth of Sarah Davis
1815	Birth of Joseph Winterhalder
	Marriage of Johannes Ganter and Magdelena Beha
1816	Birth of George Thomas Bedford
1817	Birth and death of Gertrudis Kirner
	Birth of Maria Ganter
	Birth of Heinrich Karl Ludwig Hack
1818	Birth of Amelia Motton Hunt
1819	Birth of Anton (Hepting from 1826)
1822	Marriage of Helena Kirner to Michael Brugger
	Death of Justina (Heitzman) Kirner
1824	Marriage of Agatha Kirner to Johannes Baptista Haas
	Birth of Monika Brugger
1825	Marriage of Robert Hearn to Sarah Sophia Stephenson
1826	Marriage of Lorenz Hepting to Gertrud Kirner

1831	Birth of John William Hearn
	Marriage of Joseph Nunn and Mary Parsons
1833	Birth of Mary Ann Binstead
1834	Birth of Mary Ann Nunn
	Birth of John Hardy
	Birth of Sarah Elizabeth Sharpless
	Marriage of George Thomas Bedford and Amelia Motton Hunt
1835	Death of Joseph Kirner
	Birth of Mary Jane Robbins
	Birth of George William Richard Bedford
1843	Marriage of Anton Hepting (born Kirner) to Maria Ganter
1844	Birth of Justina Hepting
1845	Marriage of Monika Brugger to Joseph Winterhalder
1846	Birth of Sophia Hepting
	Birth of Joseph Jaeggle
	Death of Johannes Ganter
1849	Death of Sophia Hepting
	Birth of Anton (Anthony) Hepting
	Birth of Sophia Winterhalder
1851	Birth of Bernhard Hepting
	Birth of Louisa Ann Hack
	Birth of Karl Spitz
	Death of Monika (Brugger) Winterhalder
	Death of Sophia Winterhalder
	Death of Magdelena (Beha) Ganter
1853	Birth of Maria Hepting
	Birth of Maria Tritschler
1854	Marriage of John Hearn to Mary Ann Nunn
	Marriage of George W R Bedford to Sarah Elizabeth Sharpless
	Death of Joseph James Nunn
1855	Birth of Markus (Mark) Hepting
	Death of Sarah Sophia (Stephenson) Bedford
1856	Birth of Amelia Adelaide Hearn
1857	Death of Helena (Kirner) Brugger
1858	Death of Agatha (Kirner) Haas
	Birth of Joseph William Hearn
	Birth of Alois Hepting
	Marriage of Michael Brugger to Isabelle Strub

1859 Death of Lorenz Hepting
Death of Johannes Baptista Haas
1861 Birth of Robert Richard Bedford
1862 Birth of Mary Jane Hearn
Death of Joseph William Hearn
Death of Amelia Adelaide (Hunt) Hearn
Death of Robert Sharpless
1863 Birth of Kate E Godson
Marriage of John Hardy to Mary Jane Robins
1864 Birth of Sarah Hearn
Birth of Emily Elizabeth Hearn
1866 Birth of Kate Florence Hardy
Birth of Ludwina Hettich
1867 Birth of Ellen Hearn
Death of Amelia Motton (Hunt) Bedford
1872 Marriage of Anthony Hepting to Louisa Ann Hack
Death of Robert Hearn
1873 Birth of Isabella McCullum
Birth of Henry James Woolner
Birth of Anthony William Hepting
1875 Birth of Louisa Christina Hepting
Birth of Caroline Alice Hollis
1876 Birth of Albert Mark Hepting
1877 Marriage of Justina Hepting to Joseph Jaeggle
1878 Marriage of Bernhard Hepting to Maria Tritschler
Birth of Bernhard Jaeggle
Birth of Maria Hepting
1880 Birth of Johanna Jaeggle
1881 Marriage of Maria Hepting to Karl Spitz
Birth of Herman Adolph Hepting
Birth of Anna Hepting
1883 Death of Maria (Ganter) Hepting
Birth and death of Freiderich Spitz
1884 Birth of Maria Wilhemina Spitz
1885 Birth of Frank Sidney Hepting
Birth of Justina Jaeggle
Birth of Karolina Hepting
Birth of Juditha Spitz

1887	Birth of Andreas Hepting
	Death of Sarah Davis
1888	Marriage of Alois Hepting to Ludwina Hettich
	Birth of Frank Hull Dyson
	Marriage of Robert Richard Bedford to Emily Elizabeth Hearn
	Birth of William George Robert Bedford
	Birth of Leopold Hepting
	Birth of Karolina Spitz
1890	Birth and death of Amanda Spitz
	Birth of Annie Elizabeth Bedford
1891	Birth of Johannes Hepting
	Birth of Ida Hepting
	Birth of Bertie Thomas Saunders
1892	Death of Anton Hepting (born Kirner)
1893	Birth and death of Antonius Hepting
	Birth of Anna Spitz
	Birth of William John Bedford
1894	Birth of Bernhard Hepting
1895	Birth of Albert Hepting
1896	Marriage of Louisa Christina Hepting to Henry James Woolner
	Death of Sarah Elizabeth (Sharpless) Bedford
1897	Marriage of Anthony W Hepting to Isabella McCullum
	Death of Mary Ann (Nunn) Hearn
	Birth of Harry Woolner
	Birth of John (Jack) Victor Bedford
1899	Birth of George Joseph Bedford
1901	Death of Markus (Mark) Hepting
	Marriage of Herman Adolph Hepting to Kate Florence Hardy
	Birth of Winifred Christine Woolner
1902	Birth of Emily Carter
	Birth of Sidney William Charles Hepting
1903	Death of Frank Sidney Hepting
	Birth of Frank Anthony John Herman Hepting
	Marriage of Albert Mark Hepting to Caroline Alice Hollis
	Birth of Louisa Frances Hepting
1904	Birth of Emily Adelaide Bedford
1905	Birth of Albert Hepting
1906	Birth of Dorothy Rose Woolner

1906	Birth of Rose Adelaide Sykes
1907	Birth of William Bernard Hepting
	Birth of Thomas Roland Dorcey
	Death of John William Hearn
1908	Birth of Charles James Bedford
1909	Birth of Dorothy Winifred Hepting
	Birth of Janet Florence Louise Hepting
	Death of Albert Hepting
1910	Birth of Lilian Rose Lucy Cartwright
1911	Birth of Harry Hepting
1913	Birth of Norman Frank Woolner
	Birth of Frederick W C Sewell
1916	Death of Louisa Ann (Hack) Hepting
	Death of Harry Woolner
	Birth of Dorothy Hilda Harvey
1917	Death of John Hardy
1920	Death of George William Richard Bedford
	Death of Anthony (Anton) Hepting
1921	Birth of Maud Kathleen Prosser
1922	Birth of Walter Woodroffe
1923	Marriage of Sidney W C Hepting to Emily A Bedford
	Birth of Sidney Robert Hepting
1924	Death of Mary Jane (Robbins) Hardy
	Birth of Stanley Rayner
1925	Birth of Emily Margaret Hepting
1927	Birth of Stanley Victor Hepting
1929	Birth of Vilma Kilrow
	Death of Isabella (McCullum) Hepting
1930	Birth of Frank Terence Hepting
	Marriage of Anthony William Hepting to Kate E (Godson) Moore
1931	Death of Caroline Alice (Hollis) Hepting
1932	Marriage of William B Hepting to Lilian Rose Lucy Cartwright
	Death of Bertie Thomas Saunders
1933	Birth of Leslie Charles Hepting
	Birth of Barbara Lilian Ward
	Birth of Sarah J Murphy
1934	Birth of James William Hepting
	Birth of Victor Bernard Hepting

1934	Marriage of Dorothy Winifred Hepting to George Baxter
	Death of Emily Elizabeth (Hearn) Bedford
1935	Birth of Frank Saville
	Birth of Thomas Pickley
1936	Birth of Ronald Edward Hepting
	Marriage of Janet Florence L Hepting to Frederick W C Sewell
	Birth of George W Newson
	Death of John William Bedford
1937	Death of Herman Adolph Hepting
	Marriage of Frank A J H Hepting to Emily Carter
	Marriage of Dorothy Rose Woolner to Thomas Roland Dorcey
1938	Birth of Ann Barbara Hepting
	Birth of June Letchford
	Birth of Joan Sewell
	Marriage of Norman Frank Woolner to Dorothy Hilda Harvey
1939	Birth of Sylvia Gwendolyn Hepting
1940	Death of Henry James Woolner
	Death of Albert Mark Hepting
	Birth of Beryl Rosemary Hepting
	Birth of Ruby Moles
	Death of Kate E (Godson) (Moore) Hepting
1941	Marriage of Harry Hepting to Maud Kathleen Prosser
	Birth of Doreen Holmes
1942	Birth of Ronald Frank Hepting
	Marriage of Winifred Christine Woolner to Frank Hull Dyson
	Marriage of Emily Margaret Hepting to Walter Woodroffe
	Birth of Kenneth Roy Hepting
1943	Death of Anthony William Hepting
	Birth of Raymond Douglas Hepting
	Birth of Jean McMahon
1945	Birth of Bernard Alexander
	Birth of Brenda Turner
	Birth of Jean Pavelin
1947	Birth of June R Foote
1948	Birth of Frederick J C Sewell
	Birth of Jean Smith
	Death of Robert Richard Bedford
	Marriage of Frank Terence Hepting to Vilma Kilrow

1950	Birth of Janet Sewell
	Birth and death of Marlene Patricia Hepting
1951	Marriage of Stanley Victor Hepting to Barbara Lilian Ward
1955	Marriage of Joan Sewell to Stanley Rayner
1957	Marriage of James William to Doreen Holmes
	Marriage of Victor Bernard Hepting to June Letchford
1958	Death of Emily (Carter) Hepting
	Marriage of Sidney Robert Hepting to Sarah J Murphy
1959	Marriage of Beryl Rosemary Hepting to George Newson
	Marriage of Ronald Edward Hepting to Ruby Moles
	Marriage of Ann Barbara Hepting to Frank Saville
	Marriage of Sylvia Gwendolyn Hepting to Thomas Pickley
1962	Marriage of Kenneth Roy Hepting to Jean McMahon
1963	Death of Kate Florence (Hardy) Hepting
	Marriage of Frank A J H Hepting to Rose Adelaide (Sykes) Sims
1964	Death of Louisa Christina (Hepting) Woolner
	Marriage of Ronald Frank Hepting to Anne Marriott
1966	Marriage of Bernard Alexander Hepting to June Foote
	Death of Frederick W C Sewell
1967	Death of Dorothy Rose (Woolner) Dorcey
	Marriage of Leslie Charles Hepting to Jean Pavelin
1968	Death of Sidney William Charles Hepting
1969	Marriage of Frederick J C Sewell to Jean Smith
	Death of William George Robert Bedford
1970	Death of Norman Frank Woolner
	Death of Annie Elizabeth (Bedford) Saunders
1972	Death of Rose Adelaide (Sykes) (Sims) Hepting
	Marriage of Kenneth Roy Hepting to Roula Michael
	Death of Charles James Bedford
1973	Death of Frank Hull Dyson
	Marriage of Leslie Charles Hepting to Doreen Wilsher
1976	Marriage of Raymond Douglas Hepting to Brenda Turner
1978	Marriage of Beryl Rosemary Hepting to Robert Campbell
	Death of George Joseph Bedford
1979	Death of Frank Anthony John Herman Hepting
	Death of Harry Hepting
1981	Death of William Bernard Hepting
1984	Death of Emily Adelaide (Bedford) Hepting

1985	Marriage of Bernard Alexander Hepting to Mary Warren
1994	Death of Winifred Christine (Woolner) Dyson
1995	Death of Lilian Rose Lucy (Cartwright) Hepting
1997	Death of Dorothy Winifred (Hepting) Baxter
1998	Death of Maud Kathleen (Prosser) Hepting
1999	Death of Stanley Victor Hepting
	Death of Raymond Douglas
2001	Death of Thomas Roland Dorcey
	Death of Louisa Frances Hepting
	Death of Sidney Robert Hepting
2002	Death of Janet Florence Louise (Hepting) Sewell
	Death of Victor Bernard Hepting
	Death of Frank Terence Hepting
2008	Death of Kenneth Roy Hepting
2009	Death of Stanley Rayner
2010	Death of Sarah Jane (Murphy) Hepting
	Death of Leslie Charles Hepting
2011	Death of Emily Margaret (Hepting) Woodroffe
2012	Death of Walter Woodroffe
	Death of Frank Saville
2013	Death of Ronald Frank Hepting
	Death of George W Newson
2014	Death of James William Hepting
	Death of Ruby (Moles) (Hepting) Chidzey
2017	Death of Dorothy Hilda (Harvey) Woolner
	Death of Barbara Lilian (Ward) Hepting
	Death of Vilma (Kilrow) Hepting
2018	Death of Bernard Alexander (Monty) Hepting
2019	Death of Beryl Rosemary (nee Hepting) (Newson) Campbell
2020	Death of Ronald Edward Hepting
	Death of Ann Barbara (Hepting) Saville

Resources and Further References

German Archives
Landesarchiv Baden-Wurttemberg Staatsarchiv Freiburg

Birth, marriage, death, census, electoral and military records
https://www.ancestry.co.uk
https://www.familysearch.org/en/
https://www.freebmd.org.uk
https://discovery.nationalarchives.gov.uk
Public Record Office at Kew, London

Ordering birth, marriage and death certificates
https://www.gov.uk/order-copy-birth-death-marriage-certificate

Searching for and ordering copies of Wills
https://www.gov.uk/search-will-probate

Finding a grave
https://www.findagrave.com

General information
https://en.wikipedia.org/wiki/Johann_Baptist_Beha

Lisbeth Seguin's book
The Black Forest: Its People and Legends, first published in 1879.

Cuckoo clocks of the Black Forest
https://www.collectorsweekly.com/articles/not-your-grandmas-cuckoo-decapitating-rat-eating-clocks-of-the-black-forest/